Andrew Lloyd Webber's

The
PHANTOM
of the
OPERA
COMPANION

PAVILION

CONTENTS

AN INTERVIEW WITH

ANDREW LLOYD WEBBER

Interviewer: First of all could you tell the story of how the present film version came about?

Andrew: Going right back to the opening of *Phantom* on Broadway in 1988, it was very clear that it was going to be a great success. Warner Brothers became very interested in making a new film version and we discussed possible directors. I had seen *The Lost Boys*, which Joel Schumacher had directed, and thought it a very visually impressive film. Joel and I got on very well and we knocked up a screenplay together, which, incidentally, is not far removed from that which we've just filmed. Then, due to personal reasons and a concern that a film would damage the proliferation of the stage show, the project got put on hold.

Ten years later Joel and I had dinner and I said to him, "what about *The Phantom of the Opera*. Don't you think it's time now?" Joel just said "yes".

Interviewer : How nervous were you about producing the film?

Andrew: The biggest single thing I had to explain is that the work is basically all song ... we were fighting a culture that had no thought that a musical could work on the big screen – there simply hadn't been one for such a long time. Then *Chicago* came along and proved that there was an interest in musicals being filmed again. With Joel we had a director who has a fantastic eye and possesses a fantastic ear for music, he understands it, he understands why you can't just cut material. This understanding was one of the greatest joys of working with Joel.

Below: *Andrew Lloyd Webber on set with Joel Schumacher during the making of the film. The pair first met in the 1980s, when Lloyd Webber asked Schumacher to direct the film version of* The Phantom of the Opera *after watching Schumacher's cult hit* The Lost Boys. *They subsequently became great friends.*

Interviewer: How important was it to you that the three leads were vocally up to the task?

Andrew: Well it's absolutely crucial of course... In Emmy, we found a seventeen-year-old girl who comes from The Metropolitan Opera School, and has got a fantastic voice. We cast Patrick Wilson, who is one of the great natural lyric tenors from the theatre, and Gerry Butler, who's got a great rock tenor voice. The vocal balance between the Phantom and Raoul was pivotal to the audiences' understanding of the characters; when they see the film they think, "I get it, I know why Christine really fancies the Phantom – I know because he's the right side of danger." It was actually a very fortunate piece of casting all the way round.

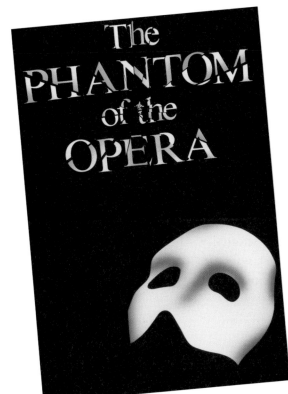

Interviewer: Finally then, could you talk about how pleased are you are with the finished film?

Andrew: It looks and sounds fabulous ... it's an extraordinarily fine document of the show. I just don't see how it could have been any better. It's a fantastic movie, I think it stands in it's own right. Of course, it's a different thing from the stage show but it doesn't threaten the integrity of the show in any way. It's taken the same material and made it into a wonderful film version. It's not at all based on the theatre visually or direction wise, but it's still got exactly the same essence ... if anything it's expanded it and given it perhaps an even deeper emotional centre.

Above: *The original poster for the stage play, which premiered in London's West End at Her Majesty's Theatre on 9 October 1986. Opening on Broadway at Majestic Theatre on 26 January 1988, it has since become the largest grossing stage or screen production in the world with a worldwide box office total of more than $3.2 billion.*

PHANTOM'S EARLY INCARNATIONS

"When I began to ransack the archives of the National Academy of Music, I was at once struck by the surprising coincidences between the phenomena ascribed to 'the ghost' and the most extraordinary and fantastic tragedy that ever excited the minds of the Paris upper classes; and I was soon led to think that this tragedy might reasonably be explained by the phenomena in question."

Taken from the opening paragraphs of Gaston Leroux's
The Phantom of the Opera

THE CREATION OF A LEGEND

Above: *Gaston Leroux just before his untimely death in April 1927.*

Left: *The cover of the first edition of Gaston Leroux's novel, published in 1911. Gaston turned to novel writing after giving up his career in journalism. Despite it's lack of initial success, the novel went on to guarantee Leroux's immortality after being turned into the 1924 film starring Lon Chaney as the Phantom.*

Fittingly, the author of *The Phantom of the Opera* novel, a classic tale of the bizarre, began life unconventionally. On 6 May 1868, his parents were on their way from Le Mans to their home in Normandy. They had to change trains in Paris, and it was here that Marie-Alphonsine went into labour. She was immediately rushed to a house, where she gave birth to a baby boy.

Years later, the young Leroux returned to Paris, looking for the house. He found an undertaker's business: "There, where I sought a cradle, I found a coffin."

The child, christened Gaston Louis Alfred, was raised in Normandy, spending much of his time in the coastal village of St Valéry-en-Caux. After acquiring his baccalaureate at Caen, he was sent to Paris to begin law studies, but already he was writing short stories and poems.

In 1889, the year he gained his law degree, his father died and left him a million francs, a sizeable sum. Young Leroux succumbed to temptation, managing to squander the money on drink, gambling and unwise speculations inside six months.

Faced by the need for an income, but hating the practice of law, he applied for a post on *L'Echo de Paris*, a paper that had already printed some of his verses. His legal training made him a good courtroom reporter and soon he was offered a better position on the important daily newspaper, *Le Matin*. This offered him scope for investigative writing, which was rapidly becoming his forte.

On one occasion, he achieved an extraordinary scoop: pretending to be a prison psychologist, he was allowed to interview a prisoner who had been remanded for a serious crime. He then wrote a brilliant article that conclusively demonstrated the man's innocence, to the discomfiture of the court officials and police.

Master of disguise

Le Matin was quick to promote their acclaimed reporter and he became a roving correspondent, travelling far and wide – across Europe and into Russia, Asia and Africa. Frequently adopting disguises, he was able to get to the heart of what would turn out to be a good story. He went with President Faure on a state visit to the Tsar. He reported the notorious second trial of Captain Dreyfuss. He stood in the crater of an erupting Vesuvius. He was the only European eyewitness of the riots in Fez. He observed the Black Sea mutinies and the rioting in Odessa and St Petersburg. He revealed to the world that the Tsar had held a secret summit with Kaiser Wilhelm II in the Baltic – a scoop he acquired by ingratiating himself with a cook in the Russian court. His adventures resulted in colourful, dramatic and entertaining copy, and his articles enhanced the circulation of the newspaper to such an extent that Leroux himself became a celebrity.

And then, in 1907, he threw it all in. Soon after returning from a long foreign assignment, his editor rang him at 3 a.m. with another assignment: to rush to Toulon where a French battleship had been damaged in an explosion. "Oh shit!" he bellowed down the phone and hung up. At that moment, he decided to become a full-time novelist.

Above and right: *Designed by architect Charles Garnier, the Paris Opéra was inaugurated on 5 January 1875 after fourteen years of construction work. The gala opening, attended by distinguished guests of the French government and the President of the Republic, Marshal McMahon, as well as King Alfonso XII of Spain and his mother, Queen Isabella, marked the beginning of a glorious era of cultural excitement, elegance and high living that was to become known as "La Belle Epoque".*

The first of Leroux's books had appeared in 1903, to be followed quickly by three more. The first, *The Seeking of the Morning Treasures*, was serialized in *Le Matin*. It was, however, *The Mystery of the Yellow Room*, published in 1907, which justified his decision to give up journalism. It was an early example of a locked room mystery, in which a murder is committed behind impenetrable sealed doors. The central character, detective Joseph Rouletabille, was to appear in seven novels.

In 1908, Leroux moved from Paris to Nice. He was by now a relatively prosperous man of letters, although the gaming tables meant that he never became really rich. Gambling was for him one of life's pleasures, and if he lost heavily, he knew that he could draw on his writing talent to furnish another book and another publisher's advance with which to write off his debt. "I work only under contract," he said. "I have to be pushed by deadlines." His son later revealed that he had the disconcerting habit of signifying the completion of a manuscript by firing a loaded revolver from his balcony.

ROMANCE, FANTASY AND HORROR

He was not merely a detective story author; his novels, published at the rate of at least one a year, embraced romance, fantasy and horror. He was also a playwright. Yet, somehow he was a man perfectly of his own time, and is now largely a forgotten figure. Hardly any of his books are in print, although when they first appeared they were very quickly issued in English translations. Several were made into films in the silent era and there were four productions of *The Mystery of the Yellow Room*, the latter two in 1930 and 1948, as talkies.

The book that guaranteed his immortality, *The Phantom of the Opera*, was published in 1911 and attracted very little attention in the first weeks. Leroux claimed to have been inspired to write the story after visiting the Paris opera house and roaming through its lower depths, inspecting the underwater lake that lies deep beneath the stage. Leroux also remembered an unfortunate accident in 1896, when one of the chandelier's counterweights had fallen on the audience, crushing one woman to death. The opera house itself had taken fourteen years to build, a fact that offered certain possibilities. Leroux realized that a well-placed person with a serious architectural background would have had the time and opportunity to create within the complex honeycomb of passages and chambers all manner of secret routes, known only to himself. Thus he gave Erik, the Phantom, the training and vocation of an architect, as well as his passion for music.

FACT AND FICTION

Leroux began his book with an introduction in which he insisted that the Opéra ghost really existed. The subsequent narrative was based on that assumption, the author assembling various documentary items and a mass of background detail to give the story a convincing air of verisimilitude. Leroux may well have invented the "faction" style of novel writing, in which real characters, events and places are interspersed with the fictional elements of the narrative with such precision that the join between truth and imagination is blurred.

Above right: *Lon Chaney's Phantom was the first visualization of Leroux's infamous character. His horrific make-up caused women to faint and his performance set a precedent for how the Phantom was later to be performed.*

Right: *A 1925 lobby card for Carl Laemmle's film version. The premiere was on 26 April 1925 in San Francisco. After it had taken place, it was decided to withdraw the print and re-edit the film to introduce some comic moments, delivered by comedian Chester Conklin. The East Coast backers felt the film now made little sense so the entire film was re-edited once again and a new set of title cards hastily produced.*

Certainly, it gained a large readership, carried as a newspaper serialization in France, Britain and the United States. Illustrations of the Phantom at his organ or swinging on the chandelier also grabbed attention. Even so, *The Phantom of the Opera* might have become as neglected as most of his other works had it not been selected as a vehicle for Lon Chaney in 1924 and filmed by Universal in Hollywood. Both the film and Chaney's performance made an extraordinary impact. Happily, Leroux lived long enough to enjoy the renewed fame the film brought him.

On 15 April 1927, at the age of fifty-nine, he died unexpectedly. He was buried in the Castle Cemetery, set high above Nice, overlooking the golden city and the azure Bay of Angels.

Lon Chaney's Phantom

In 1922, "Uncle" Carl Laemmle, president of Universal Pictures, travelled to Europe. In Paris, he met Leroux and confessed to him how excited he had been gazing at the opera house from the Place de l'Opéra. Leroux, sensing some interest, gave Laemmle a copy of *The Phantom of the Opera* for his bedtime reading. Apparently Laemmle

CARL LAEMMLE presents
"The Phantom of the Opera"

with
LON CHANEY
MARY PHILBIN
NORMAN KERRY
A. GIBSON GOWLAND
EDWIN CAREWE
and 5000 others

From the novel by
GASTON LEROUX

Directed by
RUPERT JULIAN

UNIVERSAL'S MASTERPIECE

stayed awake that night, intent on getting through the entire story. By the next morning, he had determined that it should be made into a film, but one that could be shot back home in the Universal Studios rather than in Paris. In those days, it was cheaper to build a replica of the Paris Opéra on a stage in a Californian film studio than to send a cast and crew to Europe. In any case, his company was already committed to another Paris story, *The Hunchback of Notre Dame*, and a huge outdoor set was under construction on the backlot, including a monstrous replica of the cathedral.

The star of that film, playing the misshapen Quasimodo, was Lon Chaney, whose ability to undergo fearsome physical deformation for his roles had already earned him a legendary reputation. He was a master of make-up, "the man of a thousand faces", and although his appearances were frequently grotesque, he was able to project a degree of pathos and win the sympathy of his audiences.

Playing opposite Chaney was Mary Philbin, a twenty-one-year-old former beauty queen in the role of the singer who is obsessed by the Phantom. Norman Kerry played Raoul de Chagny, with Arthur Edward Carewe as a mysterious character, Ledoux, who alone knows the truth about the Phantom.

A CHEQUERED PRODUCTION HISTORY

It was decided that the principal set of the film was to be the opera house itself, and the replica was built on Stage 28 at the Universal Studios. So sound was its construction that it stands to this day.

Shooting of the film began in 1924, but did not proceed either smoothly or harmoniously. For much of the time, intermediaries had to negotiate between the star and the first director, who were scarcely on speaking terms.

Ten weeks after filming began, Laemmle ordered that director Rupert Julian be replaced by Edward Sedgwick, an action and comedy director. It was he who shot the mob and chase scenes at the climax of the film. Following previews, he was asked to add a new subplot, which was removed *after* the premiere and replaced with comic scenes, which were themselves removed when the film's backers complained.

The 1925 release prints showed signs of the massive tinkering the film had undergone. Some sequences, such as the opening ballet and the masked ball, were shot in the old two-colour Technicolor process, which required greatly enhanced lighting, but the rest of the film was in black-and-white with occasional use of tinted stock.

Given such a chequered production history, it is surprising that the film could have turned out so well. That it did, and became a major box-office hit of the year in America, was largely on the strength of Chaney's performance, which overcame the glaring continuity lapses. Chaney had astutely arranged for a contractual clause prohibiting the use of any photographs of his Phantom make-up before the film was released. The result was a *tour de force* that struck terror throughout the audience.

Chaney's make-up was not based on a mask but on his real face. He used a wire device to push his nostrils apart and give it an upturned look. He changed the shape of his face using celluloid discs inside his cheeks. Eye drops gave him a bulging, pop-eyed look.

Left: *Mary Philbin as Christine cowers from the Phantom. The actress had been given her first break by Erich Von Stroheim in* The Merry-go-round. *Phantom was her most notable film and, with the advent of talking pictures, her career rapidly declined.*

The massive in-door set, which includes this stairwell into the Phantom's lair, still stands on Stage 28 at Universal City. The set has been used many times since – for Ronald Colman's Academy award-winning A Double Sting, *Alfred Hitchcock's* Torn Curtain *in 1966 and* The Sting, *with Robert Redford, in 1973. A tour of Universal City includes Stage 28 on its itinerary and has been visited by thousands of people over the years.*

Left: *A publicity card for another Universal production of* Phantom, *this time made with the new Technicolor film. Directed by Arthur Lubin, the film made many alterations to Leroux's novel. For example, the scene depicted in the card – the Phantom cutting the chandlier's chain – is brought forward in the story and occurs before Christine is taken down to the Phantom's lair and urged to sing for him.*

Also memorable were the set designs. Most of them were the work of Charles D. Hall, but Bart Carre designed the subterranean sets, including the Phantom's lair with his coffin-shaped bed. The chandelier's fall was achieved by lowering it slowly on a rope while an undercranked camera focused on it. When the film was played at normal speed, the chandelier appeared to fall at a lethal rate.

In 1930, following the talking picture revolution, dialogue sequences were shot for *The Phantom of the Opera* with Mary Philbin and Norman Kerry, and music and sound effects were added to the whole film. Advertised with the line "Talking! Singing! Dancing! Sound Effects! Music! Colour!", it enjoyed a new lease of life.

OTHER VISIONS

The Phantom of the Opera is a story that has enjoyed many retellings. In 1943, Claude Rains played the Phantom in a film made in glorious Technicolor. Conceived as a musical spectacular, it blunted the more frightening aspects of the story – a fact noted by the critics. The public, however, loved it, perhaps responding to its lavish production values, unusual in the economic climate of the Second World War.

In 1962, Herbert Lom played the Phantom for Hammer films, a company with a reputation for cheaply made horror films. The setting was moved to London, a city of gaslight and cobbles, and the Phantom was now a wholly sympathetic character, blamed for the foul deeds of a new menace, the Dwarf. He died attempting to save the heroine from the falling chandelier, a change to the story that robs it of dramatic tension. Not surprisingly, the film received poor critical notices.

PHANTOM GOES TO HOLLYWOOD

More successful was a 1974 television movie, *Phantom of Hollywood,* which took as its setting not an opera house, but a movie studio. The Phantom was an old, disfigured actor, played by Jack Cassidy, who had hidden out on the lot for thirty years. When the bulldozers come to destroy his home, he goes on the rampage. It's a witty idea that seems to have been dreamed up to find dramatic possibilities in the destruction of sets on the huge MGM backlot at Culver City, which was going on at the time. Several old Hollywood names also appear in it, including Broderick Crawford, Peter Lawford, Corinne Calvet, Jackie Coogan and John Ireland.

A television movie nearer to the Universal *Phantom* was broadcast in the United States by CBS in January 1983. The setting this time was Budapest before the First World War, and filming took place in Hungary, using a convenient warren of tunnels under a brewery. The Phantom was played by Maximilian Schell, with Jane Seymour as his victim and Michael York as her lover.

ROCK AND POP PHANTOM

A more interesting film variant was Brian De Palma's rock version, *The Phantom of the Paradise,* released in 1974. Much of the music was composed by Paul Williams, who also appeared as Swan, a Machiavellian record impresario. For his new rock palace, the Paradise, he steals from Winslow Leach (William Finley), taking his music on a Faust theme. After being framed, Winslow is sent to Sing Sing. He escapes, breaks into Swan's record factory to carry out sabotage, but gets his head stuck in a disc-pressing machine. To hide his deformity, he adopts a birdlike mask and a long cape, and haunts the Paradise more or less openly until persuaded by Swan to complete his rock opera on the Faust legend. Winslow agrees on condition that the lead goes to Phoenix, a girl singer (Jessica Harper) with whom he is infatuated. Swan, however, secretly assigns the part to Beef (Gerrit Graham), a gay musclebound male. The Phantom kills him and then discovers that Swan is planning to have Phoenix assassinated on coast-to-coast television. In the Phantom's final confrontation with Swan, the television rock fans of America see their spectacular deaths instead.

Part pop-rock spectacle, part camp comic-strip send-up, the film was not a success when first released, although it did establish a cult.

It has to be noticed that all the films after Lon Chaney shy away from the premise that the Phantom was born deformed but was of high intelligence and that his psychological condition stemmed from his need to hide from the real world and create an environment in which he was the master. Scriptwriters have found it easier to deal with a normal man suffering a wrong and an accidental disfigurement. Thus the Phantom's obsession has been simplified and coarsened.

Nevertheless, Gaston Leroux's yarn survives – perhaps because it has given a great opera house in a great city the romantic legend of a ghost.

Above: *The distinguished British actor Claude Rains in the 1943 production. In director Lubin's version, the Phantom, whose real name is Erique Claudin, is disfigured when a music publisher throws a tray of etching acid in his face.*

THE PHANTOM AS A MUSICAL

"I realized that the reason I was hung up was because what I was trying to write was a major romantic story, and I had been trying to do that ever since I started my career. Then, with the Phantom, *it was there!"*

Andrew Lloyd Webber, on the writing of
The Phantom of the Opera musical

ANDREW LLOYD WEBBER'S STAGE MUSICAL

Left: *The original cast of Andrew Lloyd Webber's* Phantom *featured the actor Michael Crawford and Sarah Brightman – his then wife. Although Lloyd Webber did not write the part of Christine specifically for Sarah Brightman and other actresses were auditioned, he did have her very much in mind. Brightman was ideal for the part as she was trained in both singing and dancing – an innate advantage in a role that requires proficiency in both.*

ANDREW LLOYD WEBBER was not the first to turn Gaston Leroux's compelling story into a stage musical. There have been various attempts and in 1984 a rumbustious and unashamedly camp version of *The Phantom of the Opera* was mounted at the Theatre Royal, Stratford, East London.

The director, Ken Hill, approached the twenty-three-year-old singer-dancer Sarah Brightman, shortly to become the second Mrs Andrew Lloyd Webber, to play Christine; she had to decline because of other commitments.

Prompted by a review of the musical in the *Daily Telegraph*, Lloyd Webber contacted Cameron Mackintosh, by then already a producer of many successful shows, both in the West End and on Broadway, including Lloyd Webber's own *Cats* and *Song and Dance*.

Mackintosh arranged a screening of the Lon Chaney film of 1925 and the two men also went to see Ken Hill's production. This, they thought, could be developed into a West End success, which they would produce using real opera. Ken Hill was commissioned to do a new treatment. "There was no question of me composing the score," said Lloyd Webber. "We had something like *The Rocky Horror Show* in mind."

Later in 1984, the two men met with Jim Sharman, who had staged *Jesus Christ Superstar*, Lloyd Webber's first West End success. Sharman was not available, but told Lloyd Webber "you're missing a great romantic plot – you should compose the score."

On finding a secondhand copy of the original Gaston Leroux novel, Lloyd Webber's attitude to the material was transformed. He was especially impressed that in the novel Christine keeps her promise to return to the Phantom, at his death, the ring he entrusted to her. He also enjoyed the little touches of humour Leroux gave his Phantom – a humour the music deliberately reflects in the "Shock! Horror!" chords of the title theme.

"I was actually writing something else at the time," said Lloyd Webber, "and I realized that the reason I was hung up was because what I was trying to write was a major romantic story, and I had been trying to do that ever since I started my career. Then, with the Phantom, it was there!"

Next to come into Lloyd Webber's sights was the director. He went to New York to meet with Hal Prince, who has directed or produced many legendary musicals, including *The Pyjama Game*, *West Side Story*, *Fiddler on the Roof*, *Cabaret* and the Rice–Lloyd Webber collaboration, *Evita*. "Hal told me that what he wanted to do was a great romantic musical. I said, 'What do you think about *Phantom of the Opera*?' He said, 'It sounds terrific, what have you done?' I said, 'I haven't really done anything yet, but come and see me in England.'"

Hal Prince did and said "yes" immediately. "I don't usually say 'yes' right away. It was exactly the sort of show I wanted to do – I felt that there was a real need for a romantic show."

Prince made a pilgrimage to the Paris Opéra and spent many hours climbing over every inch of the building, from the subterranean lake to the topmost pinnacle, where he ventured along narrow catwalks unsupported by handrails and found

himself looking down on the roof of Galeries Lafayette, the city's well-known department store.

The stage designer of the *Phantom*, Maria Björnson, carried out a similar reconnaissance with her assistant, which was made even more hazardous by their taking hundreds of Polaroids to serve as a reference when it came to the set design. Previously Björnson had not designed for the mainstream commercial theatre, but her work for the English National Opera and the Royal Shakespeare Company had caught the attention of both Lloyd Webber and Mackintosh.

Right and below left: *Maria Björnson, brilliant designer with the English National Opera and Royal Shakespeare companies, designed the sets and costumes for* The Phantom of the Opera, *which was her first mainstream musical. Here, Sarah Brightman wears the blue cape designed by Björnson, which is also shown in the costume design illustration.*

SUCCESS IN THE CHARTS

As with earlier shows, Lloyd Webber decided in the spring of 1985 to test the water with a record which would encapsulate the story as he then saw it. A stylish and extravagant video accompanied the single, which was directed by Ken Russell with all his visually flamboyant skill, and in which Steve Harley, the former lead singer of the rock group Cockney Rebel, played the Phantom. The tune, "The Phantom of the Opera", was arranged as a rock number, the lyrics were specially written, and the single reached No. 7 in the charts.

Now that Andrew Lloyd Webber was hard at work composing the music for the rest of the show and determining the final shape that it would take, there were other important, even brutal creative decisions that had to be made.

The lyrics for an early draft had been written by Richard Stilgoe, an accomplished writer and musician, who had previously collaborated on *Starlight Express*. "Richard Stilgoe is a good lyricist, and knows a lot about opera," explained Lloyd Webber, "but I believed that he would not be able to do it on his own. Romance is a tightrope, and it's very hard to write. It was something that in the end was my own decision, because as a composer you must get the libretto you want."

An old friend and a giant of the musical theatre, Alan Jay Lerner, was approached for help in untangling the story. Lloyd Webber recalled Lerner's reaction: "He said, 'Dear boy, it's your best score so far. You're not in as bad trouble as you think. The main thing you must not do with this plot is to ask too many questions – because it

Right: *A dressing-room scene at Her Majesty's Theatre in London's West End. Organized chaos gives way to another perfect performance.*

Below: *More of Maria Björnson's brilliant costume designs. On the left is Christine's wedding dress and on the right are designs for the two theatre managers' costumes, Andre and Firmin.*

works!' But three weeks later he wrote to me to say that although he would love to do it more than anything, he was too ill." The great lyricist of *Brigadoon* and *My Fair Lady*, *Gigi* and *Camelot* was shortly to die of cancer.

Lloyd Webber's friend and collaborator on *Evita*, Tim Rice, was also approached, but at the time he was occupied by his new show, *Chess*, due to open in May 1986.

The lyricist eventually chosen was an unknown, found in a musical writers' competition, which, as he later pointed out, he did not even win. Charles Hart was twenty-five and inexperienced, but he had a good musical ear. He was recruited after he had written some lyrics to a tape sent to him by Andrew Lloyd Webber, who had not explained that the music was for *Phantom*. Hart modestly assumed that he was offered the job because he had the same kind of typewriter as Tim Rice.

In spite of his late arrival to the project, he immediately grasped the deep romanticism of the story and the special potency of the situation in which a talented young woman is in thrall to three male figures – her high-born lover, her deceased father and Erik, the Phantom. He worked against the clock to keep up with the flow of Lloyd Webber's music, but his own musical knowledge proved invaluable, allowing the two to communicate in the special shorthand of musicians. As a result, the lyrics were produced in just three months.

Although the new version of *Phantom* was to be closer to the Leroux story than any of the films, it was considerably adapted to heighten its dramatic effect in the

theatre. Lloyd Webber believes that the construction of a musical is one of the most important ingredients in its success. "Clearly, one of the biggest problems was the unmasking of the Phantom. In the cinema, tremendous impact can be made by virtue of a close-up shot, but we had to devise a way that would make the unmasking effective from any point in a big musical theatre. I therefore decided we had to move the moment of the unmasking to a situation where a large number of characters could react to it, rather than only Christine, as was written in the book. The book gave a perfect clue. There is a scene when Christine describes being alone with the Phantom in his lair . . . 'Presently I heard the sound of the organ; and then I began to understand Erik's contemptuous phrase when he spoke about operatic music. What I now heard was utterly different from what had charmed me up to then. His *Don Juan Triumphant* (for I had not a doubt but that he had rushed to his masterpiece to forget the horror of the moment) seemed to me at first one awful, long, magnificent sob. But, little by little, it expressed every emotion, every suffering of which mankind is capable. It intoxicated me . . .' What a marvellous opportunity! I decided that if we adapted the plot to include a performance of an opera specially composed for Christine by the Phantom, we could not only introduce a far more modern musical ingredient in the score, but could contrive a situation where the Phantom was not only unmasked in front of many characters, but on the stage of his opera house, in his own opera, in what was supposed to be his night of triumph."

LLOYD WEBBER'S ADAPTATION

Lloyd Webber further altered the plot. His decision to follow the romantic strain of the Leroux novel led to his structuring the denouement of the musical as a trio between Raoul, Christine and the Phantom. Charles Hart observed that there was no intention to follow the storyline of movie versions, nor conversely, to make it seem like a faithful BBC classic serial.

Supporting Hal Prince for the musical staging and dance sequences was Gillian Lynne, a former dancer turned choreographer and director. There is little dancing in *The Phantom of the Opera,* but Andrew Lloyd Webber had asked her to join the team, aware that she was over-qualified for the job she would do. She was attracted by the prospect of working with Hal Prince again and her presence in the team enriched the production. She studied the dance styles of the period, and taught the dancers in her small ballet chorus to hold themselves with their arms in front, the torso tilted forward, eschewing the exaggerated back postures and strained legs of the post-Russian ballet. Maria Björnson's cleverly designed costumes hung exactly like the tutus and ballet skirts of the 1880s, and audiences were to applaud the Degas-style poses.

There was disappointment for Steve Harley, who had hoped that the part of the Phantom would be his. Instead, Lloyd Webber insisted that the role should go to Michael Crawford. He had heard Crawford singing when collecting Sarah Brightman from a class held by their teacher, Ian Adam, and was impressed by his vocal range. Crawford, celebrated for his physically charged performance in the title role of *Barnum*, had sung as a boy with the English Opera Group, and was cast by Benjamin Britten in the world premiere of *Noah's Flood* and *Let's Make An Opera*. Renowned for his exacting dedication to his craft, Crawford had just gone to the West Indies, on his first holiday in four years, but after three days of frantic telephone calls from London he abandoned it to present himself to the management.

It was a brilliant casting coup. Crawford not only had the physical agility to express himself with his body when his face was shrouded by its mask and disfiguring make-up, but he was also a fearless stunt performer, having no qualms about balancing precariously on a gilded angel that soars over the audience's heads, or shooting through the dangerous stage device, the star trap. The illusionist, Paul Daniels, was brought in to devise certain magic effects to enhance Crawford's performance. The Phantom was able to shoot fireballs from a staff, to appear and disappear at will, and at the end of the show to vanish in front of the audience. Said Crawford: "It was great to be in at the beginning of something. It has been the greatest adventure of my career without a doubt, to be there as it grew."

THE CASTING

Andrew Lloyd Webber has never hidden the fact that he had his then wife, Sarah Brightman, in mind when he composed the part of Christine, but her selection for the role was not a foregone conclusion, and other actresses were auditioned. Nor was this an empty exercise: the demands of the role and Brightman's physical frailty required an understudy of comparable quality, and Claire Moon was chosen, eventually taking over as the principal Christine when, in early 1987, Sarah Brightman left the cast.

Right: Lloyd Webber delighted in faking part of a Mayerbeer-esque grand opera, "Hannibal", with a scenic elephant, a demented soprano and a chorus of slave girls, meeting head-on those who had scorned his talent for pastiche.

"The role of Christine is one of the most demanding I have ever written," said her then husband. "It involves not only being able to sing music covering an enormous range for a considerable length of time, but it also demands that the artist can dance 'on pointe'. My Christine is a member of the corps de ballet. The Phantom believes in her voice because it represents a new sound in music, purer than a conventional soprano."

Christine's transformation from dancer to singer meant that Sarah Brightman was able to use her talents in both these areas. However, it was not easy. As she explained, "The way that I use my muscles as a dancer is quite different to the way I use them as a singer. Both methods work against each other and it was hard for me to separate the two. It was essential that Christine, a ballet girl suddenly plucked from the chorus to sing a leading role, developed her voice as the plot moved on if Andrew's idea of the character was to work. I had to control my voice and develop it as Christine would have done, so I couldn't start off too strong."

It was the demands of the role that led to an agreement from the outset that no actress should sing the role of Christine for more than six performances a week – a policy that was introduced by Lloyd Webber and Rice eight years previously for the musical *Evita* and which led to some compromises in the dancing when Brightman did not perform.

The Set

The choice of London theatre was particularly sensitive. Only Her Majesty's was available, a theatre that was completed in 1897 for the actor-manager, Herbert Tree. The building in the Haymarket is an exquisite example of late-Victorian theatre architecture, and the

Right: *Michael Crawford as the Phantom in the original 1986 production.*

Below: *Andrew Lloyd Webber with Sarah Brightman and Michael Crawford during the New York production. The show opened on Broadway at Majestic Theatre on 26 January 1988 and has since played to more than 10 million people, being the second longest running musical on Broadway after* Cats.

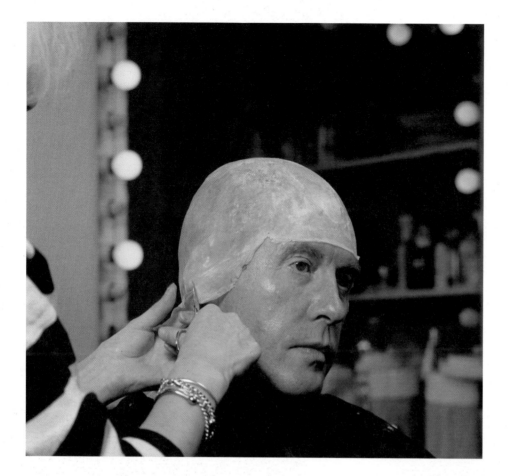

Left and below: *Michael Crawford has make-up applied. The daily procedure took approximately two hours, but before it began, Crawford's face had to be moisturized and his hair wetted down, his face shaved very closely and, every two or three days, his neck as well. Once the glue was applied to the prosthetics (the foam latex pieces that make up the Phantom's face) they could not be altered as they set in place immediately. After one hour, the make-up artist would paint, highlight and shade the Phantom's face, and two wigs would be fitted, together with the radio mike. Lastly, two contact lenses (one white and one dark blue) were put in.*

Right: *Michael Crawford sports the finished look.*

Left: *The dramatic boat scene, during the journey to the Phantom's lair.*

only house left in the West End with its original wooden machinery still intact beneath the stage. Its character was, they felt, exactly suited to the mood of the show, and Björnson incorporated some of the theatre's decorative features into her stage set, constructing a projecting rococo proscenium in front of the real one. The chandelier effect was carefully worked out. During the prologue, set at an auction on the stage of the Paris Opéra many years after the main action, the audience watch as a crumpled pile of glass and brass is hoisted aloft, transforming as it ascends into a magnificent, iridescent mass, and the scene changes to the same theatre in its heyday decades earlier. The climax of Act I brings this same chandelier plunging down to land on the stage in front of Christine, an effect achieved by a cat's cradle of invisible wires and two electric motors. The local authority inspectors scrutinized the operation of this effect to ensure that a real disaster could not happen.

Maria Björnson built the sets in miniature and displayed them in a model of the stage area. Preferring to use a model for his blocking, Prince knows in advance of rehearsals what he wants and thus he gently imposed his vision on the show. "I was watching a BBC documentary about people who were physically incapacitated … and I sensed that the thing that united them all was a very normal, healthy sexuality. And that's what Maria and I wanted to put up there, and it affected the design of the proscenium, with its statues intertwined in some moment of passion which the audiences sees and absorbs.

"It's not a simple show, but it's not an enormous technological show. We took advantage of the working Victorian machinery – we could have staged it in the same way had we opened when the theatre was first built. …We wanted to do something that would *only* work in the theatre." Andrew Bridge's magnificent lighting exactly matched that aim.

Right: *The ballet girls are instructed by Madame Giry in the original production at Her Majesty's Theatre. Their tutus were made of twelve metres of tarlatan, a kind of stiffened muslin, as were the original tutus of the Dégas period. The layers of skirt were edged using pinking scissors. The bodice was made of linen. Each girl used twelve pairs of ballet shoes per month.*

CRITICAL ACCLAIM

Few shows have generated so much anticipation, and many performances were sold out long before the opening. Advance bookings are a satisfying cushion if the critical notices turn out badly, and expensively mounted successes have often survived an initial lack of enthusiasm. Nevertheless, no producer is happy if the press is hostile.

Fortunately, *The Phantom of the Opera* impressed the critics. The duo of Michael Crawford and Sarah Brightman worked perfectly together. Crawford's discipline and energy made him seem ubiquitous, a presence pervading the atmosphere even when not on stage. His tender and hypnotic singing voice, and the tortured body movements of a man constrained emotionally and physically, gripped the audience with as powerful a hold as that of Erik over Christine. Sarah Brightman fulfilled all expectations in a role skilfully fashioned for her by her husband, and delighted the audience with the precision and clarity of her bell-like soprano.

Of the whole Company, Lloyd Webber said, "It was one of the strongest I had ever worked with. It was very exciting, as it was really the first time I had been involved with so many artists who came almost exclusively from an operatic background." The Lloyd Webber score proved to be strongly atmospheric, lushly romantic and also knowingly witty. Meeting head-on those who had scorned his talent for pastiche, he delighted in faking part of a Meyerbeer-esque grand opera,

Above left: *Mike Sterling plays the Phantom and Meredith Braun plays Christine in Spring 1999.*

Above: *The managers watch from the balcony during the 1999 Touring Production.*

Hannibal, with a scenic elephant, a demented soprano and a chorus of slave girls. The audience went home to spend days with their heads filled with some of the haunting melodies such as "Music of the Night", "All I Ask of You" and "Past the Point of No Return".

Among the many technical complications was the make-up of the Phantom. Christopher Tucker was engaged to design a horrific head that would be applied to Crawford's own features six times a week. There were endless journeys from London to Tucker's Berkshire base for a period of three months. The design had to be capable of making the audience even at the back of the upper circle recoil in disgust, without forfeiting sympathy for the misshapen Erik. At the same time, the make-up could not be so overpowering as to prevent him from acting. An inspired addition was a vertical half-mask, which left part of Crawford's face always visible. Contact lenses, however, diminished his vision to such an extent that in some scenes he had to be led on to the stage.

The physical discomfort of the double layers of latex and the wig proved to be acute. "It's like being trapped in a lift – it's quite horrendous," said Crawford. After the show had been running for a few months, he had managed to get the application stage reduced from nearly three hours to just under two.

Michael Crawford felt great sympathy for the character he created: "I feel incredibly sorry for Erik, I feel terrific compassion for him. And I think that the audience must also, because I have never seen such a reaction from men and women alike. They enjoy it in an emotional way. It's as though anyone who has ever felt love will come out crying. They feel sympathy towards that man's plea, that cry he makes at the end. Even Kate, my dresser, wept when she saw it."

Another important aspect was the physical look of Christine. The role as perceived by Lloyd Webber demanded that Christine be a convincing member of the corps de ballet – a physique which is not normally associated with operatic sopranos! As Sarah Brightman explained, "In order to prepare for the performance, I found I needed at least three hours prior to curtain up to allow me time for a complete physical, vocal and mental warm-up."

Undoubtedly, part of the success of *The Phantom of the Opera*, launched in London and destined for the world, is a consequence of the creative fusion of some of the most notable talents then at work in the theatre. But there is another factor in the success of *The Phantom of the Opera*, that of timing. Lloyd Webber's gifts include a true theatrical instinct, which allows him to sense what the public is hungry for. He wrote *Phantom* at a time when the spiky, abrasive, loose-structured musical

Right: *Celia Graham as Christine at Her Majesty's Theatre in 2002, sixteen years after the original production.*

was losing its appeal and he sensed that the public wanted romance and spectacle, proscenium arches and orchestra pits

And now, years after the Lloyd Webber *Phantom* began stalking stages across the world, he is haunting the cinema. When the idea was first suggested, Lloyd Webber was reticent. "I am a theatrical animal," he said. "But now the film has been made and who knows, it might just give us the definitive version of the Leroux legend."

FROM STAGE TO SCREEN

JOEL SCHUMACHER

Interviewer: Tell us how your involvement in *The Phantom of the Opera* film came about – with the first planned version in 1990 and then the current version?

Joel: I first met Andrew Lloyd Webber back in the late 1980s, just after I had made my fourth film, *The Lost Boys*, and he wanted to talk about the possibility of me directing the film version of *The Phantom of the Opera*. I never thought I'd get the job, but he asked me to do it and we started researching and making preparations for shooting. For various reasons the film didn't happen back then, but we stayed in touch and became friends.

We stayed close over the years and would occasionally talk about *Phantom* but I was often very busy and there were other reasons why we had to wait, so it faded into the background for a period. Then, in Christmas 2002, Andrew called me and we arranged to meet up. He asked me if I would still be interested in directing it. I remembered how exciting the whole project was years ago and I thought it would be great to make it now, so I said yes. So I guess you could say that this was about fifteen or sixteen years in the making!

It's been a very successful collaboration creatively because I take care of the filming and he takes care of the music. Andrew's company, Really Useful Films, are producing the film and helping to finance it, so I've had an enormous amount of freedom to really create what I thought should be done with the material, and I've had Andrew's full support throughout. We didn't have a third party who might have been a stranger to the project coming in so that was very helpful.

Interviewer: What was it that attracted you to the project?

Aside from the fact that visually and romantically I knew it could be an intensely powerful movie, there were two main things that appealed to me about *Phantom*: firstly it's a beautiful and profoundly tragic love story and secondly there are millions of people in the world who can't afford to go to the legitimate theatre, either because the tickets are too expensive or because it is too expensive a production to play where they live, and those things combined and gave me a huge amount of motivation.

Above: *Joel Schumacher on set with Andrew Lloyd Webber and Austin Shaw, the Executive Producer. The film took 17 weeks to shoot at Pinewood Studios, using 8 sound stages and the backlot. It took 40 weeks to construct the set, with the construction crew rising to 200 members, including carpenters, plasterers, riggers, stage hands, painters, scenic artists and sculptors.*

Andrew's music is lush and searingly romantic, and the story is a great love story, but it's also dark, it's got a Gothic horror side to it, and that appealed to me. I think above all Andrew's version really makes the Phantom much more of a tragic lover, a sensitive romantic, not just a creature of horror and fear. Christine's relationship with Raoul is really her romantic awakening as a teenager. But I think that her pull towards the Phantom is a very sexual, very deep, soulful union.

Rather than film on location, we wanted to build our own theatre because the theatre is really one of the characters in the movie, so created an opera house called the Opera Populaire. We hired a great production designer in Tony Pratt, a brilliant costume designer, Alexandra Byrne, Jenny Shircore did a fantastic job with the hair and make-up and our director of photography, John Mathieson, is a huge talent. It was a very successful collaboration of very passionate and talented people. We were able to do things that you can't do in the theatre. People really are seeing a cinematic experience of *The Phantom of the Opera*.

THE CAST

THE PHANTOM

CHRISTINE

Born in Glasgow, Gerard Butler became interested in acting from an early age, making his stage debut at the age of twelve in *Oliver*, at Glasgow's Kings Theatre. His first break came via a chance meeting in a London coffee shop with British actor and director, Steven Berkoff; after pleading for an audition, Butler landed a part in his upcoming play *Coriolanus* in London. His feature film debut came in 1998 in the Oscar-nominated Mrs Brown, in which he played Archie Brown.

Butler took singing lessons especially for the part of the Phantom, he was so determined to get the part, "by the time I got the call from Joel asking if I'd like to go and sing for Andrew Lloyd Webber I had been working really hard ... both with my own singing teacher and with Simon Lee, the music director for the film. It was a busy time ... I was shooting a film and flying back to London whenever I could to fit in more singing lessons." Butler was also greatly inspired by Patrick Wilson and Emmy Rossum, both of whom had been singing since childhood. "I had to start from scratch, but it's such a great feeling to have learned so much in one job."

Born in New York City in 1986, Emmy Rossum began her theatrical career at the age of seven, when she joined the Metropolitan Opera at Lincoln Center as a member of the Children's Chorus.

Her previous film performances include a supporting role opposite Sean Penn and Tim Robbins in *Mystic River*, and a starring role in *The Day After Tomorrow*.

Rossum almost missed the audition for the part of Christine because it coincided with a family reunion. "Someone had to make me see sense and explain what a big deal it was. I'd never seen the show, so I dashed out and bought the CD and absolutely fell in love with the music... I was drawn to the part because I recognized in Christine the emotions that I think a lot of young girls feel. She's looking for love, protection, but also for a way to express herself creatively... I don't think there's a person in the world who can't identify with at least one if not all of the three main characters. Everyone's been in love or felt unlovable, been scared, lonely or rejected. Everyone can feel for these people and the story is exciting, scary and funny."

THE CAST

RAOUL

LA CARLOTTA

Born in Virginia, USA, Patrick Wilson spent most of his childhood years in St Petersburg, Florida. An experienced Broadway performer, he first earned attention from New York audiences in the off-Broadway musical adaptation *Bright Lights, Big City*.

Wilson's previous film performances include a part in *My Sister's Wedding*, directed by David Leitner and in 2003 a starring role alongside Meryl Streep, Emma Thompson and Al Pacino in *Angels in America*.

Wilson was the first actor Schumacher cast and it was a fairly easy decision, "I knew his work. He has the looks, he's extremely talented and has the voice of an angel. He was just perfect for the part." Wilson plays the part of the dashing hero and was determined to do as much of his own stunt work in the film as possible. "I was prepared for the sword fighting because I did a lot of it in college and it was great to get the chance to use my skill. The bareback horse riding was new to me but I really wanted to do that to get across the zest for life that people at that time had."

Minnie Driver has amassed an impressive list of television and theatre credits and has built her career on diverse roles. She first came to the attention of audiences for her critically acclaimed performance in *Circle of Friends* and went on to earn an Oscar and Screen Actors Guild nomination for her performance in *Good Will Hunting*, directed by Gus Van Sant.

Driver was attracted to the *The Phantom of the Opera* and the part of La Carlotta because of the grandeur of the piece and working with Joel Schumacher. "The great thing about working with Joel is he pretty much let me do what I wanted to do. La Carlotta is a larger than life character. It's important to realize how central she is, so that when Christine takes over, we see how much of a change it is from this elaborate, passionate, crazy woman, to this beautiful young *ingénue*. La Carlotta really doesn't say much – she squarks and stomps around a lot – so we made up a lot of Italian dialogue. The skeleton was there and Joel just let me do as much as I wanted and often he wanted me to do more. He once said, 'nobody ever paid to see under the top'. That really is my character."

THE MUSIC

The original cast album of *The Phantom of the Opera*, was the first in British musical history to enter the charts at number one. Album sales now exceed forty million, and it is the biggest selling cast album of all time.

The feature film version presented the opportunity to re-visit the original recordings and, with a healthy budget to work with, Andrew Lloyd Webber realized that he could afford to produce a full orchestral version of this much loved score. The film also presented the opportunity to write a completely new song, and also several major sections of underscore to match the new screenplay. This was familiar, if slightly distant territory, having written the scores for several films early on in his career, including *The Odessa File* and *Gumshoe*.

In order to help realize this musical vision for the film Lloyd Webber turned to his trusted team. Nigel Wright, the film's music co-producer has worked with Lloyd Webber for over fifteen years, producing cast albums, video soundtracks but perhaps most pertinently the soundtrack to the 1996 film "Evita". But as Nigel explains, "Phantom's the one we've all been waiting years to do … this is the big one!" The involvement of Music Supervisor, Simon Lee, began very early. The casting process necessitates the need to work with many actors even before they see the director – Lloyd Webber was adamant that the cast had to be able to sing their own roles to a first class standard. Lee therefore began the lengthy audition and rehearsal process. Lee worked with all the principal actors, ensuring that their singing ability matched up to the high standard required. He sees his involvement at every stage as fundamental to maximizing the abilities of the cast, in particular the *Phantom*, Gerard Butler, – "Gerry was not a stage-trained singer, but sang in a band. He has been a total revelation in the last year we've been working, and I'm very proud of his achievement".

Below: *Music Supervisor Simon Lee conducts a hand-picked orchestra. Lee was central to the auditioning process and spent many months rehearsing with the principal actors.*

Above: *Nigel Wright works with Andrew Lloyd Webber in the studio set up at Abbey Road. Emmy Rossum sits behind them, Austin Shaw sits to the right.*

Shooting any musical movie has particular challenges. As Nigel Wright explains, "On every other musical movie I've made, you rehearse, then pre-record the whole soundtrack and shoot from there. What we did with Phantom was stay just one step ahead of the shooting schedule, so that the playback tracks could accommodate performances that were growing and developing during rehearsal. With construction of the huge sets running only a few weeks ahead of filming, there were times when the cast were only able to rehearse on set the week before shooting that sequence". This recording and re-recording process was continuous – a recording studio was even set up in Andrew Lloyd Webber's office at Pinewood, whereby actors could, at any time, be whisked away to record a new vocal and the playback track be altered for the next scene. It was a totally organic process for the actors and the music team alike - but this didn't come without its difficulties. "When we started, we were three weeks ahead of schedule – by the end, we were three hours ahead of what was being shot ! It would be six in the morning and we would be pre-mixing something that was going to be shot at nine!" says Wright.

The film was shot with the use of these temporary playback tracks, usually consisting of a twenty-eight piece orchestra, but on occasions where Lloyd Webber felt it necessary for the emotional drama of the piece, a full symphony line-up was used. The completion of the Director's first cut enabled Lloyd Webber and his team to assess which elements of the score would be re-orchestrated and re-recorded, and identified the need for new underscore. Working with his original collaborator, David Cullen, Lloyd Webber re-orchestrated large parts of the score, and wrote more than fifteen minutes of new music, including a fairground sequence depicting the Phantom's childhood, and a sequence for Christine's coach ride to her father's grave. A completely new song is introduced in the end credits of the film.

A hand-picked orchestra was assembled in London, many of whom were familiar with the score, having worked on stage productions, or album recordings of Lloyd Webber's work. Simon Lee conducted this orchestra at the famous Abbey Road studios - "The result is a truly sumptuous sound, exactly as Andrew had envisaged it".

PRODUCTION & SET DESIGN

Weighing in at 2.2 tons, the awe-inspiring chandelier, 17 feet high and 13.2 feet wide, is hung with some 20,000 full cut Swarovski crystal chandelier pendants. The chandelier, produced by Tisserant in Paris, took four months to construct and four days to assemble at Pinewood Studios.

The real chandelier was assembled on site and then wired up to the specially strengthened ceiling at Pinewood studios. CGI effects were used to add the chandelier to the 3-D auditorium dome. A replica stunt chandelier was used to crash down onto the stalls.

Gaston Leroux's novel *The Phantom of the Opera* is set in the Paris of the 1870s, a time – for the wealthy – of indulgence and excitement. High society flocked to the theatre and operas of 1870, particularly to the magnificent Paris Opera House. Most of the film is set in that period, but the screenplay actually begins and ends in 1919, when Raoul is an older man and returns to Paris and to the opera house. "We had to create several worlds on film," says Schumacher, "but fundamentally it can be divided into the two different time periods. The world of 1919 is quite gritty and quite real, but its still a fantasy. The 1870 period is a memory of a very romantic time lost to this old man, so that gives it a licence to be very romantic." Such a setting gave the set designer and art department plenty of scope to build a sumptuous and opulent set.

The job went to Anthony Pratt, whose film credits include *Band of Brothers* and *The End of the Affair*. "I was drawn to the film because it offered such great work for an art department: everything in the piece is so atmospheric that it's wonderful to design for and makes use of all the studio crafts, such as modelling, plasterers, carpenters and painters. This means that it becomes more enjoyable for everyone involved."

Schumacher decided to shoot the entire picture at Pinewood Studios, so the work of the designer and the art and construction departments was enormous. As Austin Shaw, the Executive Producer, explains, "Joel wanted the feel of the film to have a heightened reality to fit with the soaring gothic romance of the storyline, so we really couldn't make it on location, as the visual would jar with the story. The opera house burns down at the end of the film, so we needed to build our own – there are not many opera houses around the world who would allow us to do that – it followed that you have to build everything, to create a consistent look to the film."

*The decision to shoot the entire film on set at Pinewood Studios rather than on
location gave Production Designer Tony Pratt the chance to recreate the
figurative opulence of Garnier's original Paris Opera House. Such Rodin-
esque sculpture also appears in the auditorium and graveyard.*

The first challenge was to create a Victorian opera house, complete with seating, stage and backstage area.
Pratt, like Schumacher before him, went to Paris for inspiration: "I was lucky enough to get a tour around
the Paris Opera House by the director and so I was able to see all the backstage areas as well as well the grand
areas that the public see." The result of his research was an 886-seat theatre constructed on E stage at
Pinewood Studios. Adorned with golden statues and featuring deep red velvet upholstery, it is set off by
a golden proscenium arch leading onto the stage area beyond.

There was a further influence on Anthony Pratt's work: "Joel wanted to use the process tunnels at
Pinewood, adjacent to E stage, to build the backstage area on. That was to become the backstage and
workshop area of the theatre, a sort of labyrinthine place which would have been a hive of activity before,
during and after a performance." So Pratt and his team created a backstage world of intricate detail, not
just the dressing rooms, but also the area where the props were made, the wigs created, the armoury
cleaned and the ballet shoes kept. Building it directly next to the main stage made possible huge linking
shots following actors on and off the stage, from the public arena into the private.

Asylum, the Los Angeles-based effects house, added the necessary computer-generated imagery. The exterior
of the opera house and its surrounding buildings were built and shot as façades at Pinewood Studios. A scale
model of the opera house was built by Cinesite and superimposed later, as were the trees and buildings that
surround the opera house. The inside of the auditorium also required computer generated imagery, as the set
did not include the three-dimensional dome or the third tier of the auditorium or the Swarovski chandelier.
A plastic chandelier was used to fall from the ceiling.

COSTUME & MAKE-UP

In both stage and film mediums, *The Phantom of the Opera* offers many exciting possibilitites for costume and make-up designers. With three operas, two ballets, a masquerade ball and several love duets, there is ample opportunity to stretch one's creativity – and plenty of challenges as well.

Costume designer Alexandra Byrne, worked closely with the hair and make-up designer Jenny Shircore, a collaboration which had won acclaim for the film *Elizabeth*. A project this big required a team of two assistants, a buyer, a supervisor, a dressing team and two workrooms. The make-ups artists were split into three teams – ensemble, backstage and principals – in order to handle the large workload.

A decision was made not to stick faithfully to Victorian style. Schumacher would repeatedly remind the crew, "this is not a documentary, this is fantasy." As Shicore explains, "the research for the stage make-up of that period is thick pancake cracked make-up. But Joel wanted everything to be beautiful, so it was an interesting combination of getting a Victorian look for the period whilst also keeping it beautiful for the

modern eye." This other-worldly quality allowed Byrne to have fun, especially in designing the costumes for the diva character La Carlotta. Her deep purple "everyday" outfit (see page 94) comprised over twenty-seven metres of silk. Swarovski crystals were woven into hair and wigs. Christine is dazzling during the masquarade ball – her engagement ring, hairpieces and shimmering crystals on her dress were all custom-made by Swarovski.

The look of Lloyd Webber's Phantom has become almost iconic, with the white mask being a significant worldwide symbol. Designing it was a collaborative process involving Schumacher, Byrne, Shircore and Gerard Butler as it needed to be flexible enough for Butler to sing and move in. On the days when the Phantom was to be shot without the mask, Butler would spend many difficult hours in make-up, often starting work around 4am to be ready to go on set six hours later.

Overseeing the work at all times was Joel Schumacher. As Byrne puts it, "Joel has such a stong visual sense and knows exactly what he wants that he draws all the elements together."

THE SCREENPLAY

Scene numbers are consecutive. Where numbers have been missed out scenes have been omitted from the final film edit. Scenes remain in the correct order.

1. EXT. OPERA POPULAIRE – (1919) – DAY

We have faded into black and white film, grainy and bleak. Establishing shot of the opera house (matte shot). It is raining. The air is dank, the building grey and crumbling. There is very little activity in front. A once glorious monument shunned by the modern world.

A 1919 version of a very rich man's town car pulls up in front of the theatre: an aristocrat's family crest on the door – liveried chauffeur, a dark figure in the passengers compartment, accompanied by a nurse/nun.
> CUT TO:
a custom made, beautifully crafted, caned wheelchair is extricated from the car.
> CUT TO:
the hand made boots of the dark figure as they are adjusted into the foot rests of the wheelchair.
> CUT TO:
BACK OF NURSE … as she pushes the wheelchair toward the entrance. CAMERA goes past them and becomes their POV as we move toward the theatre. We MOVE closer; we take in statues with limbs missing, the great chipped pillars. A lackluster sign reads "Public Auction". We continue to close in; the stairs leading up to the main entrance are filthy. The place seems abandoned. We HEAR the noise of traffic; klaxons, horses but, as we MOVE closer toward the open main doors we then HEAR the <u>AUCTIONEER'S GAVEL</u>.

AUCTIONEER (O.S.)
Sold. Your number, sir? Thank you.

2. INT. FOYER – DAY

In one movement, the camera glides through the main entrance into the deserted hall revealing the vast, cracked stairway leading up to the various levels of the foyer, scarred by a fire long ago. There is rubbish everywhere. Dust floats through the shafts of grey light coming through the broken windows.

AUCTIONEER (O.S.)
Lot 663, then, ladies and gentlemen: a poster for this house's production of *Hannibal* by Chalumeau.

PORTER (O.S.)
Showing here.

We continue to move through a set of doors …

3. INT. AUDITORIUM – DAY

Also ravaged by a fire long ago … into the stalls of the auditorium. The seats are torn, even uprooted and piled on top of each other. Shafts of daylight cut through the darkness from the traps in the leaking ceiling. At the far end of the stalls in a clear space, we see a DOZEN PEOPLE grouped around the PORTLY AUCTIONEER on an improvised podium. Next to the AUCTIONEER stands a PORTER holding the poster for *Hannibal*: a diva holding a severed head.

The bidders are mainly seedy, dusty men in heavy coats; junk dealers. There is one old woman, Mme. Giry, who stands a little apart. She is dressed in black, her hat covered in black veiling like a widow. Her years as a dancer and Ballet Mistress assist her elegant and perfect posture.

AUCTIONEER
Do I have ten francs? Five then. Five I am bid. Six, seven. Against you, sir, seven. Eight? Eight once. Selling twice. Sold …

The blow of the gavel echoes around the space. The AUCTIONEER unsuccessfully tries to cover his disdain for the JUNK DEALER.

AUCTIONEER (CONT'D)
… to Monsieur Deferre. Thank you very much, sir.

The contents of the opera house are being auctioned off. We see statues, some covered with huge canvases. There are boxes, trunks, props and opera memorabilia. MME. GIRY remains stoic – mysterious; barely needing the black cane by her side. She turns to see whose POV she is.

RAOUL, the Vicomte de Chagny in the wheelchair, guided by his NURSE/NUN. Although fifteen years younger than MME. GIRY, he does not enjoy her good health. He seems small and fatigued in his beautifully tailored clothes, a cashmere throw around his barely functioning legs.

AUCTIONEER (CONT'D)
Lot 664: a wooden pistol and three human skulls from the 1831 production of *Robert le Diable* by Meyerbeer. Ten francs for this. Ten, thank you. Ten still. Fifteen, thank you. Fifteen I am bid. Going at fifteen.

MME. GIRY watches as RAOUL approaches in his wheelchair. He looks up and sees her. There is much unsaid between them, bearers of dark secrets. The GAVEL ECHOES AGAIN around the hall.

AUCTIONEER (CONT'D)
Your number, sir? Lot 665, ladies and gentlemen: a papier-mache musical box in the shape of a barrel-organ. Attached, the figure of a monkey in Persian robes, playing the cymbals. This item, discovered in the vaults of the theatre, still in working order, ladies and gentlemen.

PORTER
(Holding it up) **Showing here.** (He sets it in motion)

The simple, yet haunting tune plays as both RAOUL and MME. GIRY stare at the musical box. It has great meaning for them both.

AUCTIONEER
May I commence at fifteen francs?

MME.GIRY raises her hand.

AUCTIONEER (CONT'D) ·
Fifteen, thank you.

The NURSE raises her hand.

AUCTIONEER (CONT'D)
Yes, twenty from you sir, thank you very much.

MME. GIRY
Twenty-five.

AUCTIONEER
Twenty-five on my left, thank you madam, Twenty-five I am bid.

Again, the NURSE raises her hand.

AUCTIONEER (CONT'D)
Thirty?

MME. GIRY stares at RAOUL, her expression seems to soften. She realizes how much this means to the sickly man.

AUCTIONEER (CONT'D)
Selling at thirty francs, then.

The PORTERS whip off the canvas. The AUCTIONEER switches on the chandelier by igniting a huge battery. There is an enormous flash and the thunderous organ overture begins. The CHANDELIER, immense and glittering, begins to rise above the stalls. At the same time, a gust of wind whips up the dust and rubbish of the auditorium, almost blowing away time. CAMERA MOVES into RAOUL's eyes and we realize that the story we are about to see is in his mind.

6. INT. AUDITORIUM – (1919–1870) – DAY

As the chandelier rises, we intercut with the faces of MME. GIRY and RAOUL. The years are falling away; their features and skin are clearing, their eyes are brightening. We realize the film is GAINING COLOUR all the time. The gas lights all along the stage come on.

The red velvet seats are restored, the marble and the statues gleam, the paint glistens. The winds of time are restoring the once magnificent theatre. The chandelier is still rising, rising. We are now in FULL TECHNICOLOR. The date is 1870. FULL ORCHESTRA JOINS ORGAN: We INTERCUT the chandelier rising with:

MME. GIRY looks away.

AUCTIONEER (CONT'D)
Thirty once, thirty twice … (GAVEL DOWN) **Sold for thirty francs. To the Vicomte de Chagny. Thank you, sir.**

The box is handed across to RAOUL. He thanks MME. GIRY with his eyes, then studies the papier maché monkey.

RAOUL (V.O.)
A collector's piece indeed … every detail exactly as she said … will you still play, when all the rest of us are dead … ?

5. INT. AUDITORIUM – DAY

We CUT BACK to the AUCTIONEER as he resumes:

AUCTIONEER
Lot 666 then, a chandelier in pieces.

All attention turns to a mammoth chandelier resting on the floor of the auditorium covered in canvas. Eerie music creeps in. MME. GIRY and RAOUL can barely look to each other.

AUCTIONEER (CONT'D)
Some of you may recall the strange affair of the Phantom of the Opera: a mystery never fully explained. We are told, ladies and gentlemen, that this is the very chandelier which figures in the famous disaster. Our workshops have repaired it and wired parts of it for the new electric light. Perhaps we can frighten away the ghost of so many years ago with a little illumination. Gentlemen?

7. EXT. OPERA POPULAIRE – DAY (1870)

Establishing shot (matte) of the theatre in 1870. There is a huge activity in front of the main entrance. People queuing, milling about, staring at the vast posters for *Hannibal* starring LA CARLOTTA, the reigning diva. There are TICKET TOUTS, STREET TRADERS, BICYCLES, PEOPLE OF ALL CLASSES. LEFEVRE, the retiring manager, arrives with M. FIRMIN and M. ANDRE,

the new owners, in their carriage. They are overdressed, overfed and quite full of themselves.

9. INT. BACKSTAGE – DAY

The following montage introduces the thriving world backstage and our stock company of players. Occasionally, we see LEFEVRE, ANDRE and FIRMIN walking through. CARPENTERS and PAINTERS are preparing sections of the set in the SCENERY DOCKS. A SMALL PERSON in costume steals bread from a GYPSY and runs off. A piece of the set is rolled past on castors. Behind it TWO TUMBLERS are practicing their tricks. A bevy of BALLET GIRLS run through and up some stairs, watched closely by ANDRE and FIRMIN being shown around by LEFEVRE. Below the stairway a COSTUMED COUPLE are kissing. Above near the door an OLD MAN is sitting fast asleep. We see the COSTUME SHOPS, WIGMAKERS, PROPS, REHEARSAL HALLS, etc. The whole population of the opera house is in movement; MUSICIANS, SINGERS, DANCERS, STAGEHANDS.

10. INT. ORCHESTRA PIT – DAY

The MUSICIANS are grumbling into the ORCHESTRA PIT.

11. INT. BACKSTAGE – DAY

We see a group of SPEAR CARRIERS eating a meal around a pot. They throw food out to the DOGS waiting at the door. TWO DOGS chase each other down the corridor and crash through a half-open door watched by JOSEPH BUQUET, a sinister scene shifter in overalls. He leers as he peers through a hole in the wall; unaware of him, the youngest BALLET GIRLS are getting

changed. SEAMSTRESSES and WIGMAKERS work. GROOMS tend horses. STAGEHANDS and CARPENTERS share a bottle in the crowded BACKSTAGE AREA. BUQUET follows as a few BALLET GIRLS, including MEG GIRY – MME. GIRY's daughter – and CHRSTINE DAAE, push past him to join other girls being assembled by MME. GIRY, the severe ballet mistress, in the BACKSTAGE AREA. They are obviously late. The two young women are beautiful and innocent.

12. INT. STAGE – FLIES – DAY

We cut to a flat rising through the ropes and pulleys of the FLIES to pick up BUQUET on a ramp as a CAT runs from him, high above the stage of the opera house.

13. INT. AUDITORIUM – DAY

This entire montage of the coming to life of the 1870 Opera Populaire has been continually INTERCUT with shots of the HUGE CHANDELIER continuing to rise. Now it finds its destination, centred high above the magnificent theatre, surrounded by a painted ceiling.

14. INT. STAGE – DAY

OVERTURE ENDS as CARLOTTA's PIERCING HIGH NOTE (O.S.) crowns the moment and we CUT TO: CLOSE-UP of a dummy's severed head, mouth wide-open. CARLOTTA, in full voice, full glory and full bosom, with the rest of the COMPANY, is in mid-rehearsal for the elaborate new Meyerbeer-like production of *Hannibal*. Too much armour, fabric, glitz – all over-designed.

RAOUL (early twenties), dashing and handsome, stands in the open carriage bringing his FINE WHITE HORSES to a halt — his LIVERIED MANSERVANT jumps from his standing position on the back of the carriage as RAOUL leaps off to be fawned on and admired by the obsequious FIRMIN and ANDRE.

17. INT. STAGE – DAY

MEN'S CHORUS
The trumpets of Carthage resound! Hear, Romans, now and tremble! Hark to our step on the ground! Hear the drums – Hannibal comes!

The MEN'S CHORUS goes backstage, changes helmets and circles back to give the appearance of a larger army. PIANGI, a puffed pigeon of a baritone, enters as HANNIBAL.

PIANGI
Sad to return to find the land we love threatened once more by Roma's far reaching grasp.

REYER (TO ORCHESTRA)
Er, er, gentlemen, gentlemen, er ...

18. INT. STAGE (ANOTHER ANGLE) – DAY

LEFEVRE leads FIRMIN and ANDRE toward the stage. They continue to fawn over RAOUL.

LEFEVRE
This way. Rehearsals, as you see, are under way for a new production of Chalumeau's *Hannibal*.

The cast and stagehands turn to look at them.

REYER
Monsieur Lefevre, <u>I am rehearsing</u>!

LEFEVRE
Monsieur Reyer, Madame Giry, ladies and gentlemen, thank you – may I have your attention, please? As you know, for some weeks there have been rumours of my imminent retirement. I can now tell you that these were all true and ... it is my pleasure to introduce you to the two gentlemen who now own the Opera Populaire: Monsieur Richard Firmin and Monsieur Gilles Andre. I'm sure you have read of their recent fortune amassed in the junk business.

ANDRE
Scrap metal actually.

During this, we have cut to a moving POV from high up in the <u>FLIES</u>. We see people on the stage below. SOMEONE is watching. DARK SHADOWS move. Polite applause. Some bowing. We CUT back to the <u>STAGE.</u>

CARLOTTA
This trophy from our saviours, from our saviours, from the enslaving force of Rome!

She is holding the severed head while her MAID and SEAMSTRESS still work on her over-designed costume. The set is still under construction, PAINTERS re-touching. STAGEHANDS walk through with ladders. CARPENTERS are hammering. The conductor, M. REYER, strongly resembling Lizst, is directing her from the orchestra pit. MME. GIRY sends her BALLET GIRLS on stage. MEG and CHRISTINE among them. They are scantily and provocatively dressed.

GIRL'S CHORUS
With feasting and dancing and song, tonight in celebration, we greet the victorious throng, returned to bring salvation!

The MEN'S CHORUS enters. Now the full cast is marching and singing triumphantly.

15. INT. BELOW STAGE – DAY

We INTERCUT with the horse-driven gears below stage.

16. INT. STABLES

As the JUBILANT CHORUS rings through the entire building, FIRMIN and ANDRE excitedly rush to greet a newly arriving carriage with the DE CHAGNY family crest on the side.

FIRMIN
And we are deeply honoured to introduce our new patron.

ANDRE (beside himself)
The Vicomte de Chagny!!!

This is big news ... ooohs, aahs, applause, bowing. CHRISTINE unseen by RAOUL, goes pale.

ANDRE (to FIRMIN)
You know I still can't believe we managed to get him. It's such a coup for us my dear.

CHRISTINE (to MEG)
It's Raoul ...!

Meg turns, looks at her.

CHRISTINE
Before my father died ... at the house by the sea ... I guess you could say we were childhood sweethearts ... He called me "Little Lotte".

MEG
Oh Christine ... he's so handsome!

MME. GIRY shushes them as RAOUL, still unaware of CHRISTINE, embarrassed by the impressed, overly adoring crowd, speaks.

RAOUL
My parents and I are honoured to support all the arts, especially the world renowned Opera Populaire.

Carlotta moves forward aggressively.

LEFEVRE
Vicomte, Gentlemen, Signora Carlotta Giudicelli, our leading soprano for five seasons now.

Polite bow from ANDRE and FIRMIN. We can sense CARLOTTA is not popular with her co-workers and performers.

Carlotta curtsies.

MAID/SEAMSTRESS
Brava! Brava!

Seeing that CARLOTTA is flirting with RAOUL, PIANGI asserts himself.

LEFEVRE
And Signor Ubaldo Piangi.

Another bow.

RAOUL
An honour, signor … I believe I'm keeping you from your rehearsal. I will be here this evening to share your great triumph. (to REYER) My apologies Monsieur.

More excited reactions as RAOUL dashes off with LEFEVRE.

19. INT. STAGE – DAY

REYER (with attitude)
Thank you, Monsieur La Vicomte. (to PIANGI) Er, once more, if you please signor.

The rehearsal continues.

CARLOTTA (to MAID)
He love me. He love me.

ANDRE (to RAOUL)
Thank you, sir, thank you indeed for the wonderful words, so inspiring and encouraging. Everyone's going to get great encouragement from that. We'll do our very best, I promise…

CHRISTINE and MEG still in the midst of the waiting BALLET GIRLS.

CHRISTINE (blowing off her disappointment)
He wouldn't recognize me …

MEG
He didn't see you.

MME. GIRY
If you please.

The BALLET CORPS, including MEG and CHRISTINE, dressed scantily as slave girls, begin their dance, sure to be a crowd pleaser. ANDRE and FIRMIN move closer – they are almost hanging over MME. GIRY, leering at the ballet girls.

MME. GIRY (to FIRMIN)
Monsieur.

MME. GIRY
We take particular pride here in the excellence of our ballets, Messrs.

ANDRE
I see why. Especially that little blonde angel? (indicating MEG)

MME. GIRY
My daughter: Meg Giry.

ANDRE has an "oops" moment as FIRMIN leers on … CHRISTINE becomes prominent among the DANCERS.

FIRMIN
And that exceptional beauty? No relation, I trust?

MME. GIRY
Christine Daae. Promising talent. Monsieur Firmin, very promising.

ANDRE
Daae, did you say? No relation to the famous Swedish violinist?

MME. GIRY
His only child … orphaned at seven when she came here to live and train in the ballet dormitories …

They admire Christine's dancing and revealing costume.

FIRMIN (salivating)
An orphan, you say … ?

MME. GIRY (hands off again)
I think of her as a <u>daughter</u> also. Gentlemen, if you would kindly stand to one side?

They turn their attention to a flirtatious, toothy BALLET TART, as the ballet continues to its climax and ends. The CHORUS resumes.

CHORUS
Hannibal's friends!

CARLOTTA is getting angry. The ELEPHANT, a life-size, mechanical replica, is wheeled on. PIANGI is lifted (not easily) in triumph onto its back. The elephant's trunk suddenly rears and almost hits him. The trunk falls back down. PIANGI almost falls off. CARLOTTA steams because the new managers pay no attention to her.

CHORUS (CONT'D)
The trumpeting elephants sound – hear, Romans, now and tremble! Hark to their step on the ground – hear the drums! Hannibal comes!

Furious, CARLOTTA almost <u>screams</u> her final note in their faces.

CARLOTTA (shouts)
All they want is the dancing!

20. INT. STAGE – DAY

ANDRE, suddenly aware of CARLOTTA's rage, elbows FIRMIN, who is all over the BALLET TART, and they applaud loudly. LEFEVRE returns to join them as TWO STAGEHANDS are revealed operating the ELEPHANT from within.

LEFEVRE (to the company)
Well, the Vicomte is very excited about tonight's gala!

CARLOTTA
Ah, ah-ha-ha. Allora, allora, allora.

CARLOTTA
I hope he is as excited by <u>dancing girls</u> as your <u>new managers</u> … because <u>I</u> will not be singing!!!

She sweeps up grandly, followed by PIANGI and her entourage.

ANDRE
Lefevre … what do we do?

LEFEVRE
Grovel. Grovel – grovel.

ANDRE
Right.

ANDRE and FIRMIN dash across the stage.

FIRMIN
Signora please.

CARLOTTA
See you later because I'm going now. It is finished.

FIRMIN
World renowned artist and great beauty …

She slows down.

ANDRE
Principessa! Bella diva …

CARLOTTA
Si, si, si …

FIRMIN
Goddess of song!

CARLOTTA
Evello.

ANDRE (an idea!)
Monsieur Reyer … isn't there a rather marvellous aria for
Elissa in Act Three of *Hannibal*? Perhaps the Signora …

CARLOTTA (petulant)
Yes, yes, yes! Ma, no! Because I have not my costume for
Act Three. Because somebody not finish it!

She glares at the Russian COSTUME DESIGNER.

CARLOTTA
And, I hate my hat!

FIRMIN
But I wonder, signora, if as a personal favour, you would
oblige us with a private rendition? Unless, of course,
Monsieur Reyer objects …

CARLOTTA (flattered)
If my managers command.

FIRMIN (to CARLOTTA)
Ah.

REYER (a sarcastic bow to CARLOTTA)
My diva commands.

CARLOTTA
Yes I do. Everybody, very quiet. Sshhh!

ANDRE (starting to realize what they've gotten into)
Monsieur, why exactly <u>are</u> you retiring?

LEFEVRE (coughing and lying)
My health.

ANDRE
I see.

CARLOTTA (to CHORUS)
Sshh, sshh. You as well!

REYER
Signora?

CARLOTTA
Maestro.

The introduction is played on the piano. CARLOTTA is
performing solely for FIRMIN and ANDRE's benefit, who are
relieved and pretend to hang on every word.

CARLOTTA (CONT'D)
Think of me, think of me fondly, when we've said goodbye.
Remember me once in a while – please promise me you'll try.

During this, we <u>INTERCUT</u> between the stage and POV's from
the <u>FLIES</u>. We see the ropes starting to twitch and the pulleys

slowly loosening. There is a movement, a shadow on the ramp.

CARLOTTA (CONT'D)
When you find, that once again you long to take your heart back and be free. If you …

MEG screams. In the flies, a pulley suddenly gives. BUQUET comes out of a shadow a look of horror on his face. He rushes forward.

21. INT. STAGE ROOF – FLIES – DAY

The camera is plunging towards the stage. The ropes and pulleys are whirring madly and the counterweights shooting up towards FLIES. The counterweights hit the ramp knocking BUQUET off his feet and grabbing a rope, he also plummets downwards.

22. INT. STAGE – DAY

Camera still plunges towards CARLOTTA's head. The backdrop crashes an inch behind her.

PIANGI (looking up, furiously)
Idiot! Oh my God, signora … (to PERFORMERS) **Lift it up! Lift it up!**

Meanwhile, MME. GIRY looks up. She alone sees a <u>WHITE ENVELOPE RIMMED IN BLACK</u> fall out of the darkness above. It lands at her feet. She picks it up. She knows who it is from.

MEG (to CHRISTINE)
He's here … The Phantom of the Opera …

LEFEVRE
Signora! Are you alright?

The drop is raised high enough to reveal upstage JOSEPH BUQUET, holding a length of rope, which looks almost like a noose.

LEFEVRE (CONT'D)
Buquet! For God's sake man, what's going on up there?

BUQUET (spoken)
Please, Monsieur, don't look at me: as God's my judge, I wasn't at my post. Please, Monsieur, there's no one there: or if there is, well then, it must be a ghost …

He smirks unpleasantly.

CARLOTTA's entourage try to calm her.

ANDRE (to CARLOTTA)
Signora, please … These things do happen …

CARLOTTA
For the past three years these things do happen.
(to LEFEVRE) **And did you stop them happening? No!**
(to FIRMIN and ANDRE) **And you two – you're as bad as him. "These things do happen!" Ma … until you stop these things happening, this thing does not happen! Ubaldo! Andiamo! Bring me my doggy and my boxy.**

PIANGO
Amateurs!

CARLOTTA
Bye-bye and ciao.

CARLOTTA
Now you see. Bye-bye, I'm really leaving.

CARLOTTA storms out, sweeping up her fluffy lapdog. She is followed by PIANGI and her retinue (SEAMSTRESS, HAIRDRESSER, MAID). PIANGI is caught by his cape but undoes it.

LEFEVRE (after a pause)
**Gentlemen. Good luck. If you need me I shall be in
Australia!**

He leaves. The COMPANY look anxiously at the NEW MANAGERS.
FIRMIN looks accusingly at ANDRE.

ANDRE (weakly to REYER)
Signor Giudicelli, she will be coming back, won't she?

MME. GIRY
**You think so, messieurs? I have a message, sir, from the
Opera Ghost.**

She reveals the letter with the black border. The GIRLS twitter
and twirl in fear.

FIRMIN
Oh God in Heaven, you're all obsessed!

MME. GIRY (to ANDRE/FIRMIN)
He welcomes you to his opera house –

FIRMIN
His opera house?

MME. GIRY
**– and commands that you continue to leave Box Five empty
for his use and reminds you that his salary is due.**

FIRMIN
His salary?

MME. GIRY
**Well, Monsieur Lefevre paid him twenty thousand francs a
month.**

FIRMIN
Twenty thousand francs?

MME. GIRY
**Perhaps you can afford more, with the Vicomte de Chagny as
your patron?**

Reaction to this from the BALLET GIRLS. CHRISTINE, we see, is
comforting MEG.

FIRMIN (to MME. GIRY, sharply)
**Madame, I had hoped to make that announcement public
tonight when the Vicomte was to join us for the gala.
Obviously we shall now have to cancel as it appears we
have lost our star!**

ANDRE (the optimist)
Yeah, but surely there must be a, um ...

SINGER (to ANDRE)
Understudy!

ANDRE
... understudy?

REYER (a cry)
Understudy? There is no understudy for "La Carlotta"!

FIRMIN (to ANDRE)
A full house, Andre. We shall have to refund a full house!

Pause.

MME. GIRY
Christine Daae could sing it, sir.

All attention turns to CHRISTINE.

ANDRE
What, a chorus girl? Don't be silly.

MME. GIRY
She has been taking lessons from a great teacher.

CHRISTINE looks terrified. The older BALLET GIRLS are glaring
at her.

POV from the FLIES. Someone is still watching.

ANDRE (to CHRISTINE)
Who?

CHRISTINE (uneasily)
I don't know his name, Monsieur.

MME. GIRY knows.

MME. GIRY
Let her sing for you, monsieur. She has been well taught.

ANDRE
All right. (to CHRISTINE) **Come on, don't be shy ... Come
on. Come along. Just, just ...**

REYER (after a pause)
From the beginning of the aria then, mam'selle.

The entire company watches as Christine nervously moves
centre stage:

FIRMIN
Andre, this is doing nothing for my nerves.

ANDRE
Oh, she's very pretty.

Reyer gives Christine two bars then:

CHRISTINE
Think of me, think of me fondly, when we've said goodbye. Remember me once in a while – please promise me you'll try.

Again, here, we see the stage from high up in the flies. The Phantom's POV. Someone is watching.

CHRISTINE (CONT'D)
When you find that once again, you long to take your heart back and be free, if you ever find a moment, spare a thought for me …

As she sings, we see everyone's reactions; REYER, MME. GIRY and MEG encouraging, ANDRE and FIRMIN beginning to smile, the STAGEHANDS, CHIPPIES and PAINTERS downing tools to listen, and some of the older BALLET GIRLS gnashing their teeth. Other STAGEHANDS and PERFORMERS appear in the wings to listen to CHRISTINE. The entire population of the opera house is spellbound by CHRISTINE's voice.

23. INT. STAGE – AUDITORIUM – NIGHT

The magic, glamour and majesty of a gala performance. We are moving around CHRISTINE and, as we move behind her, the light changes. We come round the other side to reveal the packed gala auditorium. REYER is conducting a full orchestra, the gas lights are flickering.

CHRISTINE is revealed in a dazzling white costume backed by a lavish Meyerbeer-like set (moon, stars, moving clouds, a waterfall) and WHITE HORSES adorned with white wings, tended by two boys – turbaned with silver masks.

CHRISTINE
We never said our love was evergreen, or as unchanging as the sea – but if you can still remember stop and think of me … Think of all the things we've shared and seen – don't think about the way things might have been … Think of me, think of me waking, silent and resigned.

24. INT. AUDITORIUM – NIGHT

We see dozens of opera glasses raised to watch CHRISTINE.

25. INT. STAGE – NIGHT

CHRISTINE
Imagine me trying too hard to put you from my mind

Camera travels from CHRISTINE to REYER – down past the musicians, through the orchestra pit …

26. INT. PHANTOM's WORLD – PHANTOM's LAIR – NIGHT

Down through the underbelly of the stage. Down, down, ever downward – into the very bowels of the ancient stone structure which is part of the canals and locks, symbiotic with the Seine river. Somewhere in the rippling watery light – a DARK CREATURE of the night thrills to her voice – he is hidden by shadows, but we know he's there.

27. INT. STAGE – NIGHT

CHRISTINE
Recall those days, look back on all those times, think of the things we'll never do. There will never be a day when I won't think of you …

28. INT. AUDITORIUM – NIGHT

During this, we see the audience. The men in tailcoats and gloves, the women in dazzling gowns and jewellery. The whole of the French aristocracy is here in the boxes, the stalls and circles. In THE ROYAL BOX sit EMPEROR LOUIS NAPOLEON III, THE EMPRESS and THEIR ENTOURAGE.

In another, we see FIRMIN, ANDRE and young RAOUL. They are all delighted, looking at the audience and CHRISTINE on stage. THE EMPEROR claps in mid-aria, giving permission to the rest of the glittering crowd. Applause, bravos. Prominent among the bravos, those of young RAOUL in Box Five. He leaps up.

RAOUL
Can it be? Can it be Christine? (shouting) *Bravo!*

We follow him as he leaves the box.

29. INT. HALLWAY OUTSIDE BOX FIVE – NIGHT

RAOUL rushes out of the box, past MME. GIRY who has been standing near it. As she closes the door, we see the number on the door: Box Five. She watches him run toward the stairs.

30. INT. FOYER – NIGHT

The foyers are empty apart from a few guards at ease and the USHERETTES waiting.

RAOUL
Long ago, it seems so long ago, how young and innocent we were. She may not remember me, but I remember her.

We INTERCUT this with CHRISTINE on stage:

31. INT. STAGE – AUDITORIUM – NIGHT

CHRISTINE
Flowers fade, the fruits of summer fade. They have their seasons. So do we. But please promise me that sometimes you will think … (cadenza) *… of me!*

There is a pause. Camera circles CHRISTINE's face and then cranes to reveal the huge audience waiting. Then, we see the EMPEROR applauding and, suddenly, the whole house erupts. This continues over:

ANDRE (to CHRISTINE)
Brava! Magnifica! Stupenda!

REYER (to CHRISTINE)
Bravo.

32. EXT. OPERA POPULAIRE – NIGHT

A MAID, CARLOTTA's maid, runs out of a door into the courtyard toward a waiting closed carriage. CARLOTTA leans into the window. The MAID reports CHRISTINE's triumph. CARLOTTA collapses back into the carriage against PIANGI. He tries to console her but she slaps him.

33. INT. BACKSTAGE – CORRIDORS – NIGHT

The audience is crowding into the backstage corridors. Among them, RAOUL trying to find CHRISTINE. There is a crush on the stairs leading up to the dressing rooms, a mixture of ARISTOCRATS (some flirting with the BALLET GIRLS), STAGEHANDS and SINGERS. Bottles of champagne are popping, flowers are being delivered. RAOUL is trying to fight his way through. Camera follows MEG, also looking for CHRISTINE, she moves into …

34. INT. BACKSTAGE – UPSTAIRS CORRIDOR – NIGHT

… a deserted part of the building. Eerie. Meg goes out of shot and the camera goes down a small STONE STAIRWAY. It leads to a small set of doors. We go through to find …

35. INT. CHAPEL – NIGHT

… CHRISTINE, in costume, kneeling in a tiny chapel. She is lighting a candle which she places in front of a plaque. Fixed to the plaque is a daguerreotype of her FATHER. There is a sculpted violin in front. (NB. Her FATHER should very vaguely resemble the PHANTOM when disguised). We notice that there are plaques all along the wall, each with a little sculpture describing the profession of the deceased member of the Opera Populaire: ballet shoes, instruments, etc. CHRISTINE kneels to pray. She hears:

PHANTOM'S VOICE (O.S.)
Brava, Brava, Bravissima …

And a phrase on the violin. CHRISTINE looks up, drawn to the sound.

36. INT. BACKSTAGE – UPSTAIRS CORRIDOR – NIGHT

MEG is still searching for CHRISTINE.

MEG
Christine … Christine …

She sees the little stairway leading to the chapel.

37. INT. CHAPEL – NIGHT

PHANTOM'S VOICE (O.S.)
Christine …

But MEG has arrived in the chapel, giving CHRISTINE a start.

MEG (enthusiastic)
Where in the world have you been hiding? Really you were perfect! I only wish I knew your secret! Who is your great tutor?

CHRISTINE (slowly)
Meg … When your mother brought me here to live …

38. INT. OPERA POPULAIRE, FOYER – FLASHBACK – NIGHT

Dark. Empty. A seven-year-old CHRISTINE, accompanied by MME. GIRY, arrives at the Opera House. They are both in black. Someone is watching from the shadows.

CHRISTINE (V.O.)
Whenever I would come here alone to light a candle for my father …

39. INT. CHAPEL – NIGHT

Young CHRISTINE on her knees lighting the candle in the chapel. When she hears a haunting voice.

CHRISTINE (V.O.) (CONT'D)
A voice from above …

CAMERA TRAVELS above the small chapel to see a shape of a shadow singing to CHRISTINE through an elaborate filigreed grill.

CHRISTINE (V.O.) (CONT'D)
And in my dreams … he was always there.

40. INT. BALLET DORM – NIGHT – FLASHBACK

THE YOUNG CHRISTINE sleeps in the BALLET DORM – the bed next to YOUNG MEG's. She wakes to a MAGICAL VOICE. She is enthralled and inspired. CAMERA TRAVELS through a small round window that leads …

41. EXT. OPERA ROOF – NIGHT – FLASHBACK

… to the MAGNIFICENT STATUES ON THE ROOF that overlooks all of Paris. The dark silhouette sings and plays the violin …

CHRISTINE (V.O.) (CONT'D)
You see … When my father lay dying …

42. INT. SMALL BEDROOM/SEASIDE COTTAGE FLASHBACK – DAWN

CHRISTINE's FATHER dying in his small bed, whispering to the YOUNG CHRISTINE. A YOUNGER MME. GIRY watches sadly, from a distance.

CHRISTINE (V.O.)
He told me I would be protected by an Angel … an Angel of Music …

43. INT. CHAPEL – NIGHT

MEG
Christine … do you believe? … Do you think the spirit of your great father is coaching you …?

CHRISTINE
Who else, Meg? Who …??? (Distracted) *Father once spoke of an angel … I used to dream he'd appear … Now, as I sing, I can sense him … and I know he's here …* (trance-like) *Here in this room he calls me softly … somewhere inside … hiding … Somehow, I know he's always with me… He – the unseen genius …*

MEG moves toward her and begins to lead her out of the chapel.

MEG
Christine, you must have been dreaming. Stories like this can't come true … Christine, you're talking in riddles and it's not like you …

44. INT. BACKSTAGE CORRIDOR – NIGHT

[This is actually part of the stage] MEG is leading CHRISTINE down the corridor.

CHRISTINE (not hearing her, ecstatic)
Angel of music! Guide and guardian! Grant to me your glory!

We see the rafters above them.

MEG
Who is this angel?

45. INT. STAGE – FLIES – NIGHT

Flies raise and lower as BUQUET, busy securing ropes, watches them, lecherously. They are unaware of his presence.

46. INT. BACKSTAGE CORRIDOR – NIGHT

BOTH
Angel of music! Hide no longer! Secret and strange angel …

CHRISTINE (darkly)
He's with me even now …

MEG (bewildered)
Your hands are cold …

CHRISTINE
All around me …

MEG
Your face, Christine, it's white …

CHRISTINE
It frightens me …

MEG
Don't be frightened …

47. INT. BACKSTAGE/DRESSING ROOM CORRIDOR – NIGHT

They arrive in the corridor and find an adoring crowd of FANS. They move through the crowd towards CHRISTINE's dressing room amid bravos and flowers. RAOUL sees them but cannot reach them. Meanwhile, FIRMIN and ANDRE are trying to make their way toward CHRISTINE, in high spirits, bearing champagne, and fawned over by the TOOTHY BALLET TART and an equally available CHORUS GIRL.

ANDRE
A tour de force! No other way to describe it!

FIRMIN

What a relief! Not a single refund!

ANDRE (to FIRMIN)
You know it's opera tradition to drink champagne from your star's slipper.

FIRMIN
I've never been one for tradition.

He grabs the bottle from ANDRE and swigs from it.

48. INT. CARLOTTA'S DRESSING ROOM – NIGHT

MME. GIRY ushers CHRISTINE into the room. It is filled with flowers.

MME. GIRY (CONT'D) (to CHRISTINE)
You did very well, my dear. He is pleased with you.

She hands CHRISTINE a SINGLE RED rose with a black ribbon obviously from HIM.

49. INT. BACKSTAGE/DRESSING ROOM CORRIDOR – NIGHT

RAOUL finally joins ANDRE and FIRMIN near the dressing room.

FIRMIN
Ah, Vicomte, I think we've made quite a discovery with Miss Daae!

ANDRE
Perhaps we could present her to you, dear Vicomte.

RAOUL
Gentlemen, if you wouldn't mind. This is one visit I should prefer to make unaccompanied.

He takes the champagne from FIRMIN.

RAOUL
But thank you.

They bow and move off.

FIRMIN
It would appear they've met before …

ANDRE
Yes.

50. INT. BACKSTAGE – CARLOTTA'S DRESSING ROOM – NIGHT

CHRISTINE is sitting at her mirror. It is surrounded by roses. There are candles around her. RAOUL enters:

RAOUL (spoken)
"Little Lotte let her mind wander …"

CHRISTINE is puzzled.

RAOUL
"Little Lotte thought: am I fonder of dolls … or of goblins… or shoes …"

CHRISTINE
Raoul.

RAOUL
"… Or of riddles, of frocks …"

CHRISTINE
Those picnics in the attic …

RAOUL
"…Or of chocolates …"

CHRISTINE
Father playing
the violin …

RAOUL
As we read to each other
dark stories of the North …

They embrace and laugh.

CHRISTINE
"No – What I love best, Lotte said, is when I'm asleep in my bed, (sung) *And the angel of music sings songs in my head!'"*

BOTH
"*… The angel of music sings songs in my head!'*"

CHRISTINE (turning in her chair to look at RAOUL)
Father said, "When I'm in heaven child, I will send the Angel of Music to you." Well, father is dead, Raoul, and I <u>have</u> been visited by the Angel of Music.

RAOUL
No doubt of it. And now we go to supper!

CHRISTINE (firmly)
No, Raoul; the Angel of Music is very strict!

RAOUL
I shan't keep you up late!

CHRISTINE
No, Raoul …

RAOUL
<u>You</u> must change. <u>I</u>'ll order my carriage. Two minutes – Little Lotte.

He hurries out, closing the door.

CHRISTINE (calling after him)
Raoul! No, wait!

57. EXT. CORRIDOR – NIGHT

We are close on her DRESSING ROOM DOOR – A PERFECTLY GLOVED HAND turns the key in the outside door. Removing the key, the hand disappears. CAMERA TRACKS to find MME. GIRY watching from the shadows.

58. INT. CARLOTTA'S DRESSING ROOM – NIGHT

Unaware of this, and while thunderous music swells, CHRISTINE has started changing into her dressing gown. Tremulous music. CHRISTINE turns and hears the PHANTOM'S VOICE, seemingly through the timbers of the theatre.

PHANTOM'S VOICE (O.S.)
Insolent boy! This slave of fashion, basking in your glory! Ignorant fool! This brave, young suitor, sharing in my triumph!

59. INT. BACKSTAGE – NIGHT

The angry sound of the PHANTOM's voice is heard by some; MEG, MME. GIRY, BUQUET.

60. INT. FOYER – NIGHT

Dark. Empty.

60A. INT. AUDITORIUM – STAGE – NIGHT

Shots showing the opera house closed down for the night; the LAMPLIGHTERS extinguishing the lights along the stage, doors closing etc …

61. INT. BACKSTAGE – DRESSING ROOM CORRIDOR – SAME

Dark. Empty.

62. INT. BACKSTAGE/CARLOTTA DRESSING ROOM – SAME

CHRISTINE (spellbound)
Angel! I hear you! speak – I listen … stay by my side, guide me!
Angel, my soul was weak – forgive me … Enter at last, Master!

PHANTOM's VOICE
Flattering child, you shall know me, see why in shadow I hide!
Look at your face in the mirror – I am there inside!

Very dimly, behind the mirror, we begin to glimpse the white of the PHANTOM's mask over CHRISTINE's reflection. Slowly, through the following, the shape becomes more and more defined.

CHRISTINE (ecstatic)
Angel of Music! Guide and guardian! Grant to me your glory!
Angel of Music, hide no longer! Come to me, strange angel …

PHANTOM
I am your Angel of Music … Come to me Angel of Music …

CHRISTINE, mesmerized in a Svengali/Trilby-like hypnotic trance, is drawn towards the glass.

63. INT. BACKSTAGE/DRESSING ROOM CORRIDOR – NIGHT

RAOUL has returned. He hears the voices and is puzzled. He tries the door. It is locked.

RAOUL (spoken)
Whose is that voice … ? Who is that in there … ?

64. INT. BACKSTAGE/CARLOTTA DRESSING ROOM – NIGHT

Inside the room, the PHANTOM beckons to CHRISTINE from inside the mirror. She is in such a TRANCE, all we see is like a dream. He extends his hand through the mirror.

PHANTOM
I am your Angel of Music …

RAOUL (O.S.)
Christine! Christine!

PHANTOM
Come to me: Angel of Music …

Spellbound, CHRISTINE magically takes his hand and glides through the mirror.

65. INT. PHANTOM'S WORLD/CORRIDOR – NIGHT

Led by the PHANTOM, CHRISTINE has stepped into the PHANTOM's world. We are in CHRISTINE's mind now, and we experience his world from her POV. This is not the same way this world will look when MEG and the lynch mob at the end of the film see it. In her mind, it's all magic. The narrow HALLWAY they first enter is SHIMMERING, REFLECTIVE and lit by TORCHES held by HUMAN HANDS.

CHRISTINE
In sleep, he sang to me. In dreams, he came … That voice which calls to me and speaks my name …

66. INT. PHANTOM'S WORLD/STAIRCASE – NIGHT

CHRISTINE and the PHANTOM are moving down a voluptuous, spiral staircase down into the belly of the building. The walls here are covered with huge opera posters. The PHANTOM carries a torch.

CHRISTINE
And do I dream again? For now I find the Phantom of the Opera is there – inside my mind …

68. INT. PHANTOM'S WORLD/ UNDERGROUND TUNNELS/RAMPS – NIGHT

The PHANTOM is leading CHRISTINE, dressed in white, on the black horse. The architecture is steadily becoming more voluptuous and fantastic as they descend. Open-mouthed gargoyles stare from the walls.

PHANTOM
Sing once again with me our strange duet … My power over you grows stronger yet …

69. INT. PHANTOM'S WORLD/STAIRCASE/LAGOON – NIGHT

They arrive at the top of a wide staircase which leads straight down to the lagoon and a moored boat. The PHANTOM leads the horse down the staircase.

PHANTOM
And though you turn from me, to glance behind, the Phantom of the Opera is there – inside your mind …

The PHANTOM and CHRISTINE step into the boat and set off.

70. INT. PHANTOM'S WORLD/UNDERGROUND CANAL – NIGHT

The boat, guided by the PHANTOM, is gliding along the canal. Gargoyles and torches along the walls.

CHRISTINE
Those who have seen your face draw back in fear … I am the mask you wear …

PHANTOM
It's me they hear …

BOTH
Your/My spirit and my/your voice, in one combined: the Phantom of the Opera is there – inside your/my mind …

The gargoyles seem to sing as CHRISTINE stares at them.

71. INT. PHANTOM'S WORLD/LOCK/PHANTOM'S LAIR

They seem to have reached a wall, the end of the canal. The PHANTOM turns to CHRISTINE.

And we realize the water level is slowly descending, that we have reached a lock, one of the PHANTOM's devices.

CHRISTINE
He's there, the Phantom of the Opera …

PHANTOM
Sing for me! Sing, my angel of music … Sing, my angel … Sing my angel! Sing for me! (etc.)

She begins to vocalize strangely, her song climbing higher and higher in pitch. The water and the boat descend as her voice ascends. A curtain of water parts.

72. INT. PHANTOM'S WORLD/PHANTOM'S LAIR – NIGHT

The PHANTOM's lair is revealed to us. It is a fantastic grotto shaped like a harbour. As she reaches her final climactic note, candles magically rise through the water, <u>ALREADY ALIGHT</u>. The boat glides through the harbour.

Behind it a portcullis descends and a curtain closes in front of it. The lair surrounds the harbour. On one side we see the PHANTOM's pipe organ; all around are huge mirrors covered in dust sheets. We will also notice the PHANTOM's model of the opera house. The PHANTOM steps onto the shore, leaving CHRISTINE in the boat. He begins to light candles.

PHANTOM
I have brought you to the seat of sweet music's throne … to this kingdom where all must pay homage to music … music … You have come here, for one purpose, and one alone… Since the moment I first heard you sing, I have needed you with me, to serve me, to sing, for my music … my music …

The PHANTOM begins to lead the boat gently by a rope around the lair. He is lighting candles as he does so.

PHANTOM (CONT'D)
(Changing mood) *Night-time sharpens, heightens each sensation … Darkness stirs and wakes imagination … Silently the senses abandon their defences …*

The PHANTOM lights more candles revealing more of the lair. With the rope, he continues gently to guide CHRISTINE and the boat from the shore. She is in a trance. Mesmerized and hypnotized by this stunning, sexual master.

PHANTOM (CONT'D)
Slowly, gently night unfurls its splendour … Grasp it, sense it – tremulous and tender … Turn your face away from the garish light of day, turn your thoughts away from cold, unfeeling light – and listen to the music of the night. Close your eyes and surrender to your darkest dreams! Purge your thoughts of the life you knew before! Close your eyes, let your spirit start to soar! And you'll live as you've never lived before …

The PHANTOM has stepped into the water and walks toward the boat and CHRISTINE. This is highly sexual. She is completely in his spell.

PHANTOM (CONT'D)
Softly, deftly, music shall caress you … Hear it, feel it secretly possess you … Open up your mind, let your fantasies unwind in this darkness which you know you cannot fight – the darkness of the music of the night …

He lifts CHRISTINE out of the boat, her arms are around his neck, and is carrying her toward the shore. Their faces are very close. His love for her has consumed him.

PHANTOM (CONT'D)
Let your mind start a journey through a strange, new world! Leave all thoughts of the life you knew before! Let your soul take you where you long to be! Only then can you belong to me …

They reach the shore and the PHANTOM carries her toward a carved staircase. He lets her caress his mask, his hand reaches out to her face, travels down her neck and breasts. He carries her up the staircase which leads to a second grotto.

PHANTOM (CONT'D)
Floating, falling … sweet intoxication! Touch me, trust me …

savour each sensation! Let the dream begin, let your darker side give in to the power of the music that I write – the power of the music of the night …

73. INT. PHANTOM'S LAIR/BEDROOM – NIGHT

They step through into the second grotto. It is dominated by a huge bed in the shape of a black swan. The PHANTOM puts her down. She turns and is confronted by an AUTOMAT. This one is a life-size duplicate of herself in a wedding gown, surrounded by a mirror. It's too bizarre. CHRISTINE faints and falls back into the PHANTOM's arms. He carries her to the bed where he lays her down, tenderly and sensuously.

PHANTOM
You alone can make my song take flight – help me make the music of the night …

The PHANTOM has slowly been drawing a series of sheer curtains around the bed until, as the music resolves, the curtains obscure both him and CHRISTINE and we …

FADE TO BLACK

74. INT. BACKSTAGE/DRESSING ROOM CORRIDOR – NIGHT

Out of the blackness steps MEG GIRY. She is looking for CHRISTINE. The building is deserted, shadows everywhere. MEG is a tiny figure in the darkness, vulnerable and frightened.

MEG (whispers)
Christine …

75. INT. THEATRE – SAME

Dark. Empty.

76. INT. BACKSTAGE/CARLOTTA'S DRESSING ROOM – NIGHT

MEG steps into the dressing room. The gas light has been turned down low. She moves toward the dressing table covered in flowers. Next to it, we see her reflection in the full-length mirror. Suddenly, the gas light goes out. The rooms is plunged into darkness. Startled, she turns to the mirror and glimpses a shadow behind her reflection. Her hand reaches up, she steps to one side and suddenly the panel NEXT to the mirror swivels silently and gathers her through to the other side (i.e. we see the mechanics of what seemed at first magic). MEG has found CHRISTINE's route to the PHANTOM's world.

77. INT. PHANTOM'S WORLD/CORRIDOR – NIGHT

MEG comes into shot and sees the dressing room on the other side of the mirror. Shadows seem to follow. It is dark, damp and dangerous. A rat scampers through. A shadow appears

directly behind MEG. A hand reaches out and grabs her shoulder. MEG turns in terror. It is her mother, MME. GIRY.

78. INT. BALLET GIRLS' DORMITORY – NIGHT

Ten minutes later, BUQUET, showing off, is aping the PHANTOM, to the BALLET GIRLS (older ones included), who are dressed for bed. A length of fabric serves as his cloak and a piece of rope as the Punjab lasso. The toothy older BALLET TART and her CHORUS GIRL buddy, arrive home after a wild night with the bosses.

BUQUET
Like yellow parchment is his skin … A great black hole serves as the nose which never grew

Demonstrating the PHANTOM's method, he lassoes one of the girls. With a mixture of horror and delight, the BALLET GIRLS applaud this demonstration. BUQUET is clearly enjoying this.

BUQUET (CONT'D)
You must be always on your guard, or he will catch you with his magical lasso!

Behind BUQUET, MME. GIRY has entered with MEG.

MME. GIRY
Those who speak of what they know find, too late, that prudent silence is wise

She takes the noose from his hand, drops it around his head, and inserts his hand between the rope and his neck.

MME. GIRY (CONT'D)
Joseph Buquet, hold your tongue – keep your hand at the level of your eyes …

She pulls the rope taut. BUQUET's hand saves him from being strangled.

79. INT. PHANTOM's LAIR/LATER THAT NIGHT

The PHANTOM is seated at the organ, playing with furious concentration. He breaks off occasionally to write the music down. He still wears his evening trousers, but a loose velvet robe hangs open, revealing his well developed physique.

CHRISTINE is asleep. Beside the bed there is the musical box; THE MONKEY AND THE BARREL ORGAN. Mysteriously, it plays as CHRISTINE wakes up. The music keeps her in a half-trance as she steps out of the bed and walks toward the mouth of the grotto.

CHRISTINE
I remember there was mist … swirling mist upon a vast, glassy lake … there were candles all around and on the lake there was a boat, and in the boat there was a man …

She sees the PHANTOM sitting at his organ. His mask and hair perfect, bare chested in the flowing robe, he is once again a strong sexual presence CHRISTINE is attracted to. He is trying to finish a melody ("POINT OF NO RETURN"). As she approaches, she takes over the melody and, vocalizing, finds a solution to it. He then plays the middle section as she listens. She is behind him, very close. Together they complete the song, musically as one. The melody continues on the violin as the PHANTOM notates it on his score.

CHRISTINE
Who was that shape in the shadows … ? Whose is the face in the mask … ?

She lovingly caresses his face. He responds deeply to her touch. Almost like a lover, removing a veil, CHRISTINE takes off the mask. The PHANTOM springs up, throwing her violently to the ground and turns on her furiously. We see only a flash of his rotting face. In his wrath, he runs to the huge mirrors around the lair, tearing off the dust covers. CHRISTINE is surrounded by a hundred reflections of the PHANTOM.

PHANTOM
Damn you! You little prying Pandora! You little demon – is this what you wanted to see? Curse you! You little lying Delilah! You little viper – now you cannot ever be free! (weakening) *Damn you … curse you …* (a pause) *Stranger than you dreamt it … can you even dare to look or bear to think of me, this loathsome gargoyle, who burns in hell but secretly yearns for heaven, secretly … secretly … Christine …*

CHRISTINE is near tears. Her heart is moved by this poor man.

PHANTOM (CONT'D)
Fear can turn to love – you'll learn to see, to find the man behind the monster, this … repulsive carcass, who seems a beast, but secretly dreams of beauty, secretly … secretly … Oh, Christine …

Pitifully, he holds out his hand for the mask, and filled with sympathy, she gives it to him. He puts on the mask.

PHANTOM (CONT'D)
Come, we must return – those two fools who run my theatre will be missing you.

80. INT/EXT. ROOF (MEG'S POV) – NIGHT

… sees the spectre of the Phantom leading Christine across the roof.

81. INT. BALLET GIRLS' DORMITORY – NIGHT

MEG
He's there – the Phantom of the Opera!

The other BALLET GIRLS scream. MME. GIRY claps her hands to order the girls to bed.

MME. GIRY
Au lit! Au lit!

82. INT. BACKSTAGE/CORRIDOR – NIGHT

MME. GIRY locks the doors of the dormitory. She looks up and sees at the top of a staircase, CHRISTINE, backlit by the moon, still deep in a trance. CHRISTINE walks down towards her and almost faints into MME. GIRY's arms as she reaches her. MME. GIRY leads her away. Unknown to them both, BUQUET has been watching them. And unknown to BUQUET, from the doorway above, the PHANTOM has been watching him.

DISSOLVE TO:

83. EXT. OPERA POPULAIRE / BACK TO 1919
(BLACK AND WHITE GRAINY FOOTAGE AGAIN)

The NURSE/NUN and the LIVERIED CHAUFFEUR assist the frail RAOUL into the back of his elegant car. As the NURSE and DRIVER get seated, RAOUL looks up to see MME. GIRY leaving the theatre. As his car moves away slowly, they both look to each other – two old friends that have shared many dark secrets – who know they will probably never see each other again. With great effort, RAOUL makes a chivalrous gesture. He raises his silk top hat in respect and places it over his heart.

MME. GIRY is moved, and does a tiny, elegant curtsy. RAOUL leaving his hat off, rests back in the expensive leather seat. His mind once again fills with haunted dreams of the past. He looks in the SIDE MIRROR.

HIS POV. The old, SCARRED THEATRE disappearing in the distance. CAMERA moves in closer to his EYES as rear view BLACK AND WHITE SIDE MIRROR fills the screen and it ONCE AGAIN bursts into COLOUR and we are:

84. EXT. OPERA POPULAIRE – 1870 – MORNING

FIRMIN walks hurriedly toward the theatre, carrying a newspaper. LARGE QUEUES outside the theatre. Everybody wants a ticket.

86A. INT. GRAND FOYER – DAY

Passing CLEANERS with mops, FIRMIN enters, reading:

FIRMIN
"Mystery after gala night" it says, "Mystery of soprano's flight!" "Mystified," all the papers say, 'We are mystified – we suspect foul play!" (he lowers the paper) *Bad news on soprano scene – first Carlotta, now Christine! Still at least the seats get sold – gossip's worth its weight in gold …*

He strides towards ANDRE's office at the other end.

FIRMIN
What a way to run a business! Spare me these unending trials. Half your cast disappears, but the crowd still cheers! Opera! To hell with Gluck and Handel – Have a scandal and you're sure to have a hit!

ANDRE bursts out of his office, in a temper, confronting FIRMIN in the busy corridor.

ANDRE
Damnable? will they all walk out? this is damnable!

FIRMIN
Andre, please don't shout … it's publicity! And the take is vast! Free publicity!

ANDRE (groans)
But we have no cast …

FIRMIN (calmly)
But, Andre, have you seen the queue?
FIRMIN is now leading him back to his office ANDRE produces a black bordered letter.

FIRMIN (CONT'D)
Oh, it seems you've got one too …

88. INT. GRAND FOYER – DAY

As they march in, ANDRE opens the letter and reads:

ANDRE
"Dear Andre, what a charming gala! Christine was, in a word, sublime. We were hardly bereft when Carlotta left – on that note, the diva's a disaster, must you cast her when she's seasons past her prime?"

Meanwhile, FIRMIN has picked up another letter from his desk. It also has a black border. He reads it out:

FIRMIN
'Dear Firmin, just a quick reminder: my salary has not been paid. Send it care of the ghost, by return of post – P.T.O.: no one likes a debtor, so it's better if my orders are obeyed!'

BOTH
Who would have the gall to send this? Someone with a puerile brain!

FIRMIN (studying both notes)
They are both signed "O.G." …

ANDRE
Who the hell is he?

BOTH (immediately realizing)
"Opera ghost!"

And back down the corridor.

FIRMIN
It's nothing short of shocking

ANDRE
He's mocking our position

FIRMIN
In addition he wants money!

ANDRE
What a funny apparition …

BOTH
... to expect a large retainer! Nothing plainer – he is clearly quite insane!

They are interrupted by the arrival from the stairs of RAOUL, who brandishes another of the PHANTOM's notes.

RAOUL
Where is she?

ANDRE
You mean Carlotta?

RAOUL
I mean Miss Daae – where is she?

FIRMIN
Well, how should we know?

RAOUL
I want an answer – I take it that you sent me this note?

FIRMIN
What's all this nonsense?

ANDRE
Of course not!

FIRMIN
Don't look at us!

All three start off back towards FIRMIN's office.

RAOUL
She's not with you, then?

FIRMIN
Of course not!

ANDRE
We're in the dark ...

RAOUL
Monsieur, don't argue – isn't this the letter you wrote?

FIRMIN
And what is it that we're meant to have wrote?
(Realizing his mistake)
Written!

RAOUL hands the note to ANDRE who reads it:

ANDRE
"Do not fear for Miss Daae. The Angel of Music has her under his wing. Make no attempt to see her again."

The managers look mystified.

RAOUL
Well, if you didn't write it, who did?

90. INT. GRAND FOYER – DAY

They are just about to go into FIRMIN's office when CARLOTTA, closely followed by PIANGI and her retinue (SEAMSTRESS, MAID, HAIRDRESSER) explodes into the foyer and heads up the grand staircase. She, too, has a letter, which has cheered her no more than the others.

CARLOTTA
Where is he?

ANDRE (delighted)
Ah, welcome back!

CARLOTTA
Your precious patron – where is he?

RAOUL
What is it now?

They all go toward FIRMIN's office, as CARLOTTA confronts RAOUL.

CARLOTTA
I have your letter – a letter which I rather resent!

FIRMIN (to RAOUL)
And did you send it?

RAOUL
Of course not!

ANDRE
As if he would!

CARLOTTA and PIANGI
You didn't send it?

RAOUL
Of course not!

FIRMIN
What's going on … ?

CARLOTTA (to RAOUL)
You dare to tell me that this is not the letter you sent?

RAOUL
And what is it that I'm meant to have sent?

RAOUL takes the letter and reads it:

RAOUL
"Your days at the Opera Populaire are numbered. Christine Daae will be singing on your behalf tonight. Be prepared for a great misfortune, should you attempt to take her place."

The MANAGERS are beginning to tire of the intrigue. They escort CARLOTTA toward the grand staircase. EVERYONE has followed them.

ANDRE and FIRMIN
Far too many notes for my taste – and most of them about Christine! All we've heard since we came is Miss Daae's name…

And walk straight into MME. GIRY accompanied by MEG.

MME. GIRY
Miss Daae has returned.

FIRMIN (looking at RAOUL)
I hope no worse for wear as far as we're concerned

ANDRE
Where precisely is she now?

MME. GIRY
I thought it best she was alone …

MEG
She needed rest …

RAOUL
May I see her?

MME. GIRY
No, monsieur, she will see no one.

CARLOTTA and PIANGI
Will she sing? Will she sing?

ANDRE and FIRMIN try to escape up the stairs. EVERYONE follows.

MME. GIRY
Here, I have a note …

They all groan.

RAOUL/CARLOTTA/ANDRE/PIANGI
Let me see it!

FIRMIN (snatching it)
Please!

He opens the letter and reads. The PHANTOM's voice gradually takes over.

FIRMIN
"Gentlemen, I have now sent you several notes of the most amiable nature, detailing how my theatre is to be run. You have not followed my instructions. I shall give you one last chance …"

We INTERCUT with:

94. INT. PHANTOM's LAIR – DAY

The PHANTOM's model of the Opera Populaire. We see in particular the stage of the opera house with the set for *Il Muto*. Figurines, exact reproductions of the cast, IN WAX, CARLOTTA and CHRISTINE included, populate the stage.

The PHANTOM's hand, in a white glove, comes into shot. It removes the head from the CHRISTINE figurine and swaps it with that of CARLOTTA's.

PHANTOM's VOICE (O.S.)
(taking over) *Christine Daae has returned to you, and I am*

anxious her career should progress. In the new production of Il Muto, *you will therefore cast Carlotta as the pageboy, and put Miss Daae in the role of Countess. The role which Miss Daae plays calls for charm and appeal, the role of the pageboy is silent – which makes my casting, in a word, ideal.*

We also see Box Five within the model:

PHANTOM (O.S.)
I shall watch the performance from my normal seat in Box Five, which will be kept empty for me. Should these commands be ignored a disaster beyond your imagination will occur …

The PHANTOM's hand taps the miniature chandelier of the model opera house. We INTERCUT this with:

95. INT. AUDITORIUM – DAY

The real chandelier tinkles as if disturbed by a gust of wind.

95A. INT. BACKSTAGE – SAME

Workers look up and react to tinkling chandelier.

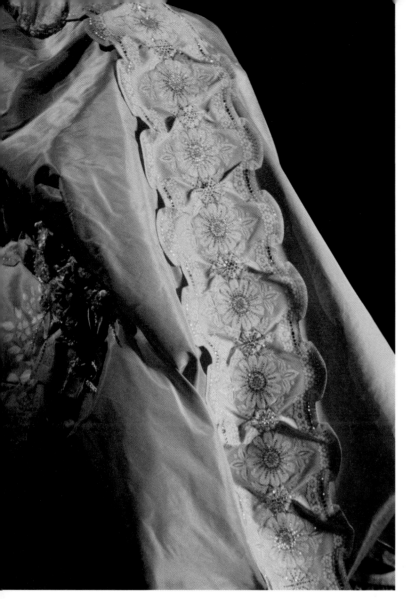

CARLOTTA plunges down the stairs followed by EVERYONE.

CARLOTTA
I know who sent this: (pointing an accusing finger) *The Vicomte – her lover!*

RAOUL (ironical)
Indeed? (to the others) *Can you believe this?*

FIRMIN
(to Carlotta, in protest) **Signora!**

She heads for the DOORS TO THE THEATRE.

98. INT. BACKSTAGE/DRESSING ROOM CORRIDOR – DAY

As EVERYONE races down the corridor, other SINGERS, DANCERS, HAIR and MAKEUP ARTISTS appear out of the dressing rooms to watch.

CARLOTTA (half to the MANAGERS, half to herself)
O traditori!

ANDRE
This changes nothing!

CARLOTTA
O mentitori!

FIRMIN
Signora!

99. INT. BACKSTAGE/CARLOTTA'S DRESSING ROOM – DAY

And they all arrive in CARLOTTA's dressing room. She is like a whirlwind: trunks and cases appear, dresses, boas, wigs, furs, shoes, fly through the air into the trunks. She is packing to leave.

ANDRE
You are our star!

FIRMIN
And always will be!

ANDRE
Signora …

FIRMIN
The man is mad!

ANDRE
We don't take orders!

FIRMIN (announcing it to everyone)
Miss Daae will be playing the pageboy – the silent role …

96. INT. GRAND FOYER – DAY

EVERYONE looks up as if they heard the distant sound of the chandelier.

FIRMIN (taking over)
" … I remain, gentlemen, your obedient servant, O.G."
CARLOTTA
Christine

CARLOTTA barrels towards the grand staircase. EVERYONE follows.

ANDRE
Whatever next … ?

CARLOTTA
It's all a ploy to help Christine!

FIRMIN
This is insane …

ANDRE and FIRMIN
Carlotta will be playing the lead!

CARLOTTA
(waxing melodramatic)
it's useless trying to appease me … you're only saying this to please me! I will not listen! You thus insult the honour of your prima donna? Padre mio! Dio!

PIANGI
… appease her … to please … her … padre mio! … padre mio! … dio!

100. INT. BACKSTAGE – DAY

<u>TIME CUT (FIVE MINUTES LATER)</u>: (CONTINUOUS MUSIC)

CARLOTTA is now starting to make her way out of the opera house. She is followed by EVERYONE, although now her retinue includes PORTERS carrying her trunks and cases.

We travel down corridors and rooms we have seen already in our initial montage presenting the opera house; the <u>COSTUME SHOPS</u>, <u>WIGMAKERS</u>, <u>PROP STORES</u>. We sweep down stairways through the <u>SCENERY DOCKS</u>. The whole population of the opera house – CARPENTERS, STAGEHANDS, DANCERS, SINGERS, PAINTERS, MUSICIANS – become aware of what is happening; LA CARLOTTA is leaving forever.

MME. GIRY
Who scorn his word beware to those … The angel sees, the angel knows …

CARLOTTA (to the MANAGERS)
You have reviled me!

101. INT. STAGE - DAY

They are all moving through the <u>WINGS</u> now.

CARLOTTA
You have rebuked me!

ANDRE and FIRMIN
Signora, pardon us …

CARLOTTA, her RETINUE, PORTERS and the OTHERS have arrived on stage in the middle of a rehearsal for *Il Muto*. SINGERS, dancers give way. REYER looks up amazed from the pit as CARLOTTA rolls centre stage and hits a high note:

CARLOTTA
You have replaced me!

102. INT. AUDITORIUM – DAY

CARLOTTA swirls down from the stage into the stalls followed by EVERYONE. ANDRE and FIRMIN attempt various pincer movements through the aisles to head her off but she will not be stopped.

ANDRE and FIRMIN
Please, Signora, we beseech you …

MME. GIRY
This hour shall see your darkest fears …

RAOUL
I must see her …

CARLOTTA
Non vo' cantar! Non vo' cantar!

CARLOTTA goes through the doors into:

103. INT. GRAND FOYER – DAY

CARLOTTA crosses the lobby.

RAOUL
Where did she go … ?

CARLOTTA
Non vo' cantar!

ANDRE and FIRMIN
Signora, sing for us! Don't be a martyr …

CARLOTTA
Non vo' cantar!

RAOUL/GIRY/MEG
What new surprises lie in store … ?

ANDRE and FIRMIN
Our star!

CARLOTTA has reached the huge MAIN DOORS LEADING OUTSIDE. And, as she hits the highest note she sweeps them open to see:

104. EXT. OPERA POPULAIRE – DAY

The ENORMOUS QUEUES of her ADORING FANS, FIRMIN had seen earlier from his office. They applaud and cheer CARLOTTA and adoringly throw roses at her pudgy feet.

FAN (to CARLOTTA)
Would you please give this to Miss Daae? Miss Daae?

105. INT. FOYER – DAY

ANDRE and FIRMIN steal behind her, close the doors and stand with their backs to them. All look at CARLOTTA, as the MANAGERS approach her lovingly.

ANDRE
Your public needs you!

FIRMIN
We need you, too!

CARLOTTA (unassuaged)
Would you not rather have your precious little ingenue?

ANDRE and FIRMIN
Signora, no! the world wants you!

106. INT. BACKSTAGE/CARLOTTA'S DRESSING ROOM – NIGHT

CARLOTTA is preparing for the evening performance of *Il Muto*. She is surrounded by her SEAMSTRESS, WIGMAKER, MAID and PIANGI.

Through the following, she is strapped into her corset, bosoms heaving, perfume, powdered, wigs and beauty spots are applied. Most importantly, she is constantly spraying her throat from a crystal bottle. Meanwhile, ANDRE and FIRMIN fawn magnificently; they have brought her bonbons, oysters, huge flowers, another nasty little dog. PIANGI groans. They drink champagne from her slipper, FIRMIN a little disgusted by this, and grovel like pros.

ANDRE and FIRMIN
Prima Donna, First Lady of the stage! Your devotees are on their knees to implore you!

We INTERCUT this with:

107. INT. BACKSTAGE/DRESSING ROOM CORRIDOR – NIGHT

… RAOUL searching for CHRISTINE. We also intercut with:

108. INT. BACKSTAGE/HUMBLE DRESSING ROOM – NIGHT

MME. GIRY is preparing a very nervous CHRISTINE as the PAGEBOY. MEG is with them.

109. INT. BACKSTAGE/CARLOTTA'S DRESSING ROOM – NIGHT

ANDRE
Can you bow out when they're shouting your name?

FIRMIN
Think of how they all adore you!

BOTH
Prima Donna, enchant us once again!

ANDRE
Think of your muse …

FIRMIN
And of the queues round the theatre!

BOTH
Can you deny us the triumph in store!

ANDRE/FIRMIN/PIANGI
Sing, Prima Donna, once more!

110. INT. BACKSTAGE/CORRIDORS – NIGHT

We continue intercutting with RAOUL searching for CHRISTINE.

RAOUL
Christine spoke of an angel …

111. INT. BACKSTAGE/CARLOTTA'S DRESSING ROOM – NIGHT

CARLOTTA (to herself in triumph)
Prima Donna, your song shall live again!

ANDRE/FIRMIN/PIANGI (to CARLOTTA)
Think of your public!

CARLOTTA
You took a snub, but there's a public who needs you!

MME. GIRY (referring to CHRISTINE)
She has heard the voice of the angel of music …

ANDRE/FIRMIN/PIANGI (to CARLOTTA)
Those who hear your voice liken you to an angel!

CARLOTTA
Think of their cry of undying support!

CONTINUE INTERCUTS (CONTINUOUS MUSIC)

112. INT. BACKSTAGE – DRESSING ROOM CORRIDOR – NIGHT

RAOUL is making his way to Box Five.

113. INT. BACKSTAGE – NIGHT

CARLOTTA, followed by her RETINUE and ANDRE and FIRMIN, PIANGI now carrying two little dogs, is now moving toward the wings. She travels past the COSTUME and PROP SHOPS, the SCENERY DOCKS, while ANDRE and FIRMIN encourage other

SINGERS and DANCERS to follow and SING her praises. CARLOTTA is continuously spraying her mouth with the little crystal bottle.

114. INT. STAGE – PIT – FLIES – NIGHT

Shots which show the theatre coming to life for the evening performance; MUSICIANS arriving in the <u>PIT</u>; BUQUET directing operations up in the <u>FLIES</u>; the huge bed of *Il Muto* being wheeled on stage.

ANDRE (to FIRMIN)
We get our opera …

FIRMIN (to ANDRE)
She gets her limelight!

115. INT. BACKSTAGE – NIGHT

BALLET GIRLS and the CHORUS dress. PROPS are readied. MEG and MME. GIRY attend CHRISTINE. (All INTERCUT with CARLOTTA and COMPANY getting ready.)

CARLOTTA
Follow where the limelight leads you!

ANDRE and FIRMIN (aside)
Leading ladies are a trial!

CARLOTTA
Prima Donna, your song shall never die!

PIANGI
When she sings we see heaven!

CARLOTTA
You'll sing again, and to unending ovation!

RAOUL
Orders! Warnings! Lunatic Demands!

ANDRE and FIRMIN
Lunatic demands are regular occurrences

CARLOTTA
Think how you'll shine in that final encore!

ANDRE and FIRMIN
Surely there'll be further scenes – worse than this!

RAOUL
… I must see these demands are rejected!

ANDRE and FIRMIN
Who'd believe a diva happy to relieve a chorus girl, who's gone and slept with the patron? Raoul and the soubrette, entwined in love's duet! Although he may demur, he must have been with her!

ANDRE and FIRMIN
You'd never get away with all this in a play, but if it's loudly sung, and in a foreign tongue, it's just the sort of story audiences adore, in fact, a perfect opera!

MME. GIRY
For, if his curse is on the opera …

MEG
But if his curse is on this opera …

ANDRE and FIRMIN
Prima Donna, the world is at your feet! A nation waits, and how it hates to be cheated!

ALL
Light up the stage with that age-old rapport! Sing, Prima Donna, once more!

116. INT. WINGS/STAGE – NIGHT

CARLOTTA and her RETINUE, ANDRE and FIRMIN, have arrived on the edge of the opera stage. They are now accompanied by other SINGERS, DANCERS, STAGEHANDS. The huge set beckons as the music rises and EVERYONE's eyes are on CARLOTTA.

THE OVERTURE TO *Il Muto*

117. INT. AUDITORIUM – NIGHT

We see the stage of the opera house. The red house curtains are in. The house is packed.

119. INT. WINGS/STAGE – NIGHT

The PERFORMERS waiting for the opera to begin. Meanwhile, in the wings, the PHANTOM's hand comes into shot. Unseen by all, it reaches for CARLOTTA's throat spray and swaps it for an identical crystal flask. The overture comes to an end and …

120. INT. AUDITORIUM – NIGHT

… the curtains rise for the beginning of the opera.

A PERFORMANCE OF *Il Muto*

121. INT. STAGE – NIGHT

The set is an eighteenth century salon, a canopied bed centre stage. The COUNTESS is played by CARLOTTA. SERAFIMO, the pageboy, is disguised as her maid and is played by CHRISTINE. At this point, they are hidden behind the drapes of the bed, which are drawn. We see them waiting for their cue. CARLOTTA yanks the cap on CHRISTINE's head, trying to cover part of her face. In the room are TWO EPICENE MEN: one a HAIRDRESSER and one a JEWELLER. The JEWELLER is attended by MEG dressed as a maid. There is also an OLDER WOMAN, the COUNTESS's CONFIDANTE. ALL, apart from MEG, are gossiping with relish about the COUNTESS's current liaison with SERAFIMO.

CONFIDANTE
They say that this youth has set my lady's heart aflame!

1ST FOP
His Lordship, sure, would die of shock!

2ND FOP
His Lordship is a laughing-stock!

CONFIDANTE
Should he suspect her, God protect her!

ALL THREE (INSINCERELY)
Shame! Shame! Shame! This faithless lady's bound for Hades! Shame! Shame! Shame!

The AUDIENCE is amused as the canopy drapes part and we see the COUNTESS kissing SERAFIMO passionately. As the recitative begins, the lights and the music dim on stage, and our attention turns to the MANAGERS in their box.

122. INT. AUDITORIUM/MANAGERS' BOX – NIGHT ON STAGE

COUNTESS
Serafimo! Your disguise is perfect! (a knock on the door) *Why, who can this be?*

DON ATTILIO (outside)
Gentle wife, admit your loving husband.

ANDRE and FIRMIN chuckle and nod to RAOUL in the opposite box. He acknowledges them.

ANDRE (to FIRMIN)
Now that's exactly the sort of thing the public loves.

123. INT. STAGE – NIGHT

The COUNTESS admits PIANGI as DON ATTILIO, an old fool.

DON ATTILIO
My love – I am called to England on affairs of state, and must leave you with your new maid. (aside) *Though I'd happily take the maid with me!*

COUNTESS (ASIDE)
The old fool is leaving!

ANDRE (to FIRMIN)
It's the Countess de Charbourg! She's invited us to her salon, you know.

FIRMIN (to ANDRE)
Nothing like that ever happened to us in the junk business.

ANDRE (to FIRMIN)
Scrap metal.

COUNTESS (CARLOTTA)
Serafimo – away with this pretence!

She rips off SERAFIMO's skirt to reveal his manly breeches.

COUNTESS (CONT'D)
You cannot speak, but kiss me in my husband's absence! Poor fool, he makes me laugh! Hahaha haha! Time I tried to get a better better half!

COUNTESS/CHORUS
Poor fool, he doesn't know! Hoho, hoho, ho! If he knew the truth, he'd never ever go!

Suddenly, from nowhere, we hear the VOICE of the PHANTOM.

PHANTOM'S VOICE (O.S.)
Did I not instruct that Box Five was to be kept empty?

MEG (terrified, whispered)
He's here, the Phantom of the Opera …

And high above the stage, on a catwalk running along the top of the proscenium arch, we can make out the shadowy figure of the PHANTOM. General reaction of bewilderment. EVERYONE stops. AUDIENCE reaction. CHRISTINE looks fearfully about her.

CHRISTINE
It's him.

CARLOTTA (finding a scapegoat in CHRISTINE, hisses at her:)
Your part is silent, little toad!

She walks off stage into the <u>WINGS</u>. There, her MAID hands her throat spray. CARLOTTA sprays herself liberally. But the PHANTOM has heard her last remark.

PHANTOM (O.S.)
A toad, madam? Perhaps it is you who are the toad …

Again general unease, this time turning to alarm. CARLOTTA comes back on stage.

CARLOTTA (to MAID)
Why you spray on my chin all the time, huh?

CARLOTTA (to REYER in the pit)
Maestro … da capo … Per favore … *Serafimo, away with all this pretence! You cannot speak, but kiss me in my husband's <u>croak</u> …*

Instead of singing, she emits a great croak, like a toad. A stunned silence. CARLOTTA is as amazed as anyone, but regains herself and continues. More perturbing, however, is a new sound: the PHANTOM is laughing – quietly at first, then more and more hysterically. The entire AUDIENCE howls.

REYER (to ORCHESTRA)
Gentlemen, please, please. Now, come along.

CARLOTTA
Poor fool, he makes me laugh! Haha, haha, <u>croak, croak, croak</u>

STAGEHAND
She's lost her voice.

As before, the PHANTOM's laughter rises. The croaking continues as the chandelier's lights flicker on and off. The PHANTOM's laughter, by this time overpowering, now crescendos into a great cry:

124. INT. AUDITORIUM DOME – NIGHT

Unseen by the audience, the PHANTOM is in the dark belfry of the opera house dome.

And with this, he toys perilously with the chandelier.

124A. INT. AUDITORIUM – NIGHT

The AUDIENCE gasps.

124B. INT. AUDITORIUM DOME – NIGHT

BUQUET appears from a trap door. He sees the PHANTOM. The PHANTOM sees him. BUQUET disappears in terror.

125. INT. STAGE – NIGHT

CARLOTTA looks tearfully up at the MANAGER's box and shakes her head.

ANDRE and FIRMIN hurry onto the stage. PIANGI ushers the now sobbing CARLOTTA off stage, while the MANAGERS tackle the audience, the chandelier still swaying wildly.

FIRMIN
Er Ladies and gentlemen, we apologize. Er, the performance will continue in ten minutes' time …

He addresses Box Five which is now <u>EMPTY</u>, keeping one eye on the chandelier as it returns to normal.

FIRMIN (CONT'D)
When the role of the Countess will be sung by Miss Daae. Thank you. (to CHRISTINE) **Go, go, hurry up, hurry up.**

FIRMIN (to AUDIENCE)
Until then, we would crave your indulgence for a few moments.

Meanwhile, we see <u>BACKSTAGE</u> the STAGEHANDS working frantically lowering the curtain and changing the set.
ANDRE (improvising)

Meanwhile, ladies and gentlemen, we shall be giving you the ballet from Act Three of tonight's opera.

REYER
What?!

ANDRE (to REYER)
Er, maestro … (stutters) … the, the, the ballet – bring it forward please.

The MANAGERS leave, the stage is cleared fast and the music starts up again. The BALLET GIRLS enter as a sylvan glade flies in. They begin the Dance of the Country SHEPHERDESSES complete with swings, a shepherd and real sheep.

126. INT. STAGE – FLIES – NIGHT

We INTERCUT the Dance with events up in the flies. The flats from the previous scene continue to move up. BUQUET is supervising from the main ramp. As one flat rises out of shot, he sees the PHANTOM on another ramp. The PHANTOM grabs a rope and leaps across towards BUQUET. We see this from both the stage below and through POV's of the stage way below us. BUQUET runs down his ramp chased by the PHANTOM who has used the ropes to swing across from ramp to ramp. Continue INTERCUTS with:

127. INT. CARLOTTA's DRESSING ROOM – NIGHT

MME. GIRY helps CHRISTINE into CARLOTTA's costume.

128. INT. STAGE – NIGHT

MEG is aware of the events above her head and dances out of step.

129. INT. CARLOTTA's DRESSING ROOM – NIGHT

CHRISTINE notices the SINGLE RED ROSE with the BLACK RIBBON.

130. INT. STAGE – FLIES – NIGHT

Finally, BUQUET turns to run from the PHANTOM but a rope like a flash catches him by the neck. Then very fast, we see the PHANTOM leap off the ramp holding a rope, BUQUET is suddenly raised straight off his feet, the noose around his neck;

a pulley whirls madly; the PHANTOM lands on a lower ramp, releases the rope. BUQUET plummets.

131. INT. STAGE – NIGHT

The garrotted body of JOSEPH BUQUET falls on the stage with a sickening thud (or stays suspended centre stage) causing the sylvan glade to fly out. Pandemonium.

132. INT. BACKSTAGE/WINGS – NIGHT

CHRISTINE is running through backstage, terrified. RAOUL runs towards her, she grabs him. She still grasps the PHANTOM's rose.

133. INT. STAGE – NIGHT

FIRMIN is attempting the impossible:

FIRMIN (trying to placate the audience)
Ladies and gentlemen, please remain in your seats.
Er, do not panic. It is simply an accident … an accident …

134. INT. BACKSTAGE/IRON STAIRCASE – NIGHT

CHRISTINE is leading RAOUL up a spiralling iron staircase which leads vertiginously out onto the roof. CHRISTINE is racing up, in a frenzy of terror.

RAOUL
Why have you brought me here?

CHRISTINE
We can't go back there!

RAOUL
We must return!

CHRISTINE
He'll kill you! His eyes will find us there!

RAOUL
Christine, don't say that …

CHRISTINE
Those eyes that burn!

RAOUL
Don't even think it …

CHRISTINE
And if he has to kill a thousand men –

RAOUL
Forget this waking nightmare …

CHRISTINE
The Phantom of the Opera will kill and kill again! (to herself)
My god, who is this man who hunts to kill ...? I can't escape from him ... I never will!

BOTH
And in this labyrinth, where night is blind, the Phantom of the Opera is here/there: inside my/your mind

RAOUL
There is no Phantom of the Opera ...

135. INT./EXT. ROOF – NIGHT

They emerge onto the roof. The huge statue of "La Victoire Ailee", vast gargoyles dominate and look out over a surreal panorama of Paris.

CHRISTINE (calming a little but intense)
Raoul, I've been there – to his world of unending night ...

RAOUL
The Phantom is a fable ... Believe me, there is no Phantom of the Opera...
(to himself)
My god, who is this man, the mask of death ... ? Whose is this voice you hear with every breath ... ?

to a world where the daylight dissolves into darkness ... Darkness ... Raoul, I've seen him! Can I ever forget that sight... ? Can I ever escape from that face? So distorted, deformed, it was hardly a face, in that darkness ... darkness ...

And we realize the PHANTOM is right there with them on the roof. He watches from the top of a statue. We INTERCUT continuously between the lovers and him.

CHRISTINE (trance-like, then becoming more and more ecstatic)
But his voice filled my spirit with a strange, sweet sound ... In that night, there was music in my mind ... And through music my soul began to soar! And I heard as I'd never heard before ...

RAOUL
What you heard was a dream and nothing more ...

CHRISTINE (still abstracted)
Yet in his eyes all the sadness of the world, those pleading eyes that both threaten and adore ...

CHRISTINE is spellbound by the PHANTOM's rose. The PHANTOM sees and hears this. He leans back, moved.

RAOUL (irritated)
Christine … Christine …

PHANTOM (unseen, a ghostly echo of love)
Christine …

RAOUL takes the rose from her.

RAOUL (almost interrupting)
No more talk of darkness, forget these wide-eyed fears. I'm here: nothing can harm you – my words will warm and calm you. Let me be your freedom, let daylight dry your tears.

Snowflakes begin to fall on the opera roof. And, as the snow slowly covers the roof and the statues, we INTERCUT between the lovers, their shadows, and the PHANTOM and his shadow to the point where the PHANTOM's shadow replaces RAOUL's.

RAOUL
I'm here with you, beside you, to guard you and to guide you …

CHRISTINE
Say you love me every waking moment, turn my head with talk of summertime … Say you need me with you, now and always … Promise me that all you say is true – that's all I ask of you …

RAOUL
Let me be your shelter, let me be your light. You're safe: no one will find you – your fears are far behind you …

The lovers move perilously close to the edge of the roof.

CHRISTINE
*All I want is freedom, a world with no more night …
and you, always beside me, to hold me and to hide me …*

A shadow. Perhaps the PHANTOM will send them to their deaths?

RAOUL
*Then say you'll share with me one love, one lifetime …
let me lead you from your solitude …*

The PHANTOM silently mouths RAOUL's words of love, his heart broken.

RAOUL (CONT'D)
Say you need me with you here, beside you … anywhere you go… Let me go too – Christine, that's all I ask of you …

CHRISTINE
Say you'll share with me one love, one lifetime … Say the word, and I will follow you …

BOTH
Share each day with me, each night, each morning …

CHRISTINE
Say you love me …

RAOUL
You know I do …

BOTH
Love me – That's all I ask of you …

They kiss. The PHANTOM is watching, heartbroken. Their intertwining shadows are next to him and in the snow.

BOTH
Anywhere you go, let me go too … Love me – that's all I ask of you …

CHRISTINE starts from her reverie.

CHRISTINE (moving off)
I must go – they'll wonder where I am … Come with me, Raoul!

RAOUL (following)
Christine, I love you!

CHRISTINE
Order your fine horses! Be with them at the door!

RAOUL
And soon you'll be beside me!

CHRISTINE
You'll guard me, and you'll guide me …

They disappear down the iron staircase back into the opera house. The PHANTOM has emerged from behind a statue where he casts a vast shadow in the fresh snow. CHRISTINE has dropped his RED ROSE with the BLACK RIBBON in the snow.

PHANTOM (very quiet and plaintive)
I gave you my music … made your song take wing … And now, how you've repaid me: denied me and betrayed me … He was bound to love you when he heard you sing … Christine …

He sinks to his knees holding the RED ROSE.

137. INT./EXT. ROOF – NIGHT

The PHANTOM hears the lovers' duet fading away below …

RAOUL AND CHRISTINE (O.S.)
Say you'll share with me one love, one lifetime … Say the word, and I will follow you … (softer, more distant) Share each day with me, each night, each morning …

He sinks to his knees as he crushes the rose in his hands.

PHANTOM (with sudden and terrifying fury)
You will curse the day you did not do all that the Phantom asked of you ... !

CAMERA pulls higher and higher.

FADE TO BLACK

138. FADE INTO: EXT./INT. PARIS STREET CAR – DAY – 1919 (BLACK AND WHITE)

RAOUL's car stops in traffic. RAOUL comes out of his memories to notice ...
    RAOUL's POV. A young couple, deeply in love, look longingly in the windows of an elegant jewellery store. RAOUL remembers his own young love as the couple moves along, revealing a dazzling display of expensive jewels.
    CAMERA moves closer and closer to the RINGS, and as it zero's into the FLASHY GEMS, hit by the late afternoon light, SCREEN fills with out of focus, EYE-POPPING brilliance which DISSOLVES into INCANDESCENT FIREWORKS in SPECTACULAR TECHNICOLOR.

139. EXT. PARIS SKY 1870 – NIGHT

CAMERA moves down to include the OPERA POPULAIRE
A spectacular explosion of fireworks in the starry sky. We descend to reveal (MATTE) a glittering opera house. It is New Year's Eve; the night of the Gala Masked Ball.

140. EXT. OPERA POPULAIRE – NIGHT

Watched by a LARGE CROWD OF ONLOOKERS held back by GENDARMES, the magnificently COSTUMED GUESTS step out of their CARRIAGES and make their way up to the main entrance. (Note: the Ball has a colour theme: Black and White/Silver and Gold).
    The stairs are lined with GUARDSMEN. PHOTOGRAPHERS take pictures of the GUESTS. The flash powder bursts. The ONLOOKERS applaud the most lavish costumes. With its torchlight façade, the whole building glitters.

142. EXT. OPERA POPULAIRE – NIGHT

FIRMIN and ANDRE greet guests as they mount the steps and take champagne from a silver tray.

FIRMIN (to ANDRE)
Monsieur Andre.

ANDRE (to FIRMIN)
Monsieur Firmin.

FIRMIN
Dear Andre, what a splendid party!

ANDRE
The prologue to a bright New Year!

FIRMIN
Quite a night! I'm impressed!

ANDRE
Well, one does one's best ...

They are joined by the TOOTHSOME BALLET TART, spilling out of her bodice and an equally SEXY GIRL from the CHORUS.

BOTH (raising their glasses)
Here's to us!

ANDRE
The toast of all the city!

FIRMIN
What a pity that the Phantom can't be here!

We follow them as they walk into ...

143. INT. FOYER – NIGHT

... and CRANE up to reveal the spectacular Opera Ball in full swing. This sequence is more of a promenade than a dance, the GUESTS revelling in their own magnificence. For all this, there is a strangely eerie aspect to the crowd, too many PHANTOM

LOOK-ALIKES and SKELETONS for comfort. There is a general movement up and down the central horseshoe staircase; a grandiose spectacle with the music.

CHORUS
Masquerade! Paper faces on parade! Masquerade! Hide your face, so the world will never find you! Masquerade! Every face a difference shade … Masquerade! Look around – there's another mask behind you!

The CAMERA picks out individual GUESTS.

CHORUS (variously)
Flash of mauve … Splash of puce … Fool and king … Ghoul and goose … Green and black … Queen and priest … Trace of rouge … Face of beast … Faces … Take your turn, take a ride on the merry-go-round … in an inhuman race … Eye of gold … Thigh of blue … True is false … Who is who? Curl of lip … Swirl of gown … Ace of hearts … Face of clown…

We see FIRMIN and ANDRE toasting each other.

CHORUS (CONT'D)
Faces … drink it in, drink it up, till you've drowned in the light … in the sound …

RAOUL and CHRISTINE have arrived in the foyer. A PHANTOM LOOK-ALIKE whizzes past.

MASKED COUPLE
But who can name the face … ?

ALL
*Masquerade! Grinning yellows, spinning reds …
Masquerade! Take your fill – let the spectacle astound you!
Masquerade! Burning glances, turning heads …
Masquerade! Stop and stare at the sea of smiles around you!
Masquerade! Seething shadows, breathing lies …
Masquerade! You can fool any friend who ever knew you!
Masquerade! Leering satyrs, peering eyes … Masquerade!
run and hide – but a face will still pursue you!*

CARLOTTA and PIANGI make a grand entrance, joined by ANDRE, FIRMIN, MEG, MME. GIRY, glasses in hand.

CARLOTTA
What a night!

PIANGI
What a crowd!

ANDRE
Makes you glad!

FIRMIN
Makes you proud! All the crème de la crème …

They have been joined by RAOUL and CHRISTINE. We can see CARLOTTA does not appreciate CHRISTINE's costume.

CARLOTTA
… Watching us, watching them!

RAOUL (to CHRISTINE)
And all our fears are in the past!

ANDRE is leading them through the foyer toward the auditorium.

ANDRE
Three months …

PIANGI
… of relief!

CARLOTTA
… of delight!

ANDRE
… of Elysian peace!

FIRMIN
And we can breathe at last!

CARLOTTA
No more notes!

PIANGI
No more ghost!

144. INT. GRAND FOYER – NIGHT

They have arrived in the festively decorated auditorium.

RAOUL
Here's to health!

ANDREW
Here's a toast: to a prosperous year!

FIRMIN
To our friends who are here.

CARLOTTA and PIANGI
And may our splendour never fade!

FIRMIN
Three months!

CARLOTTA
What a joy!

PIANGI
What a change!

ANDRE and FIRMIN
What a blessed release!

ANDRE leading them back into the foyer:

ANDRE
And what a masquerade!

INTERCUTS TO …

145. INT. BACKSTAGE – NIGHT

The WORKERS enjoy their own party.

146. INT. STABLES – NIGHT

The WORKERS enjoy their own drunken dance.

147. INT. FOYER – NIGHT

RAOUL and CHRISTINE, however, have found a corner to share a moment alone together. CHRISTINE is admiring a new acquisition: an engagement ring from RAOUL which she has attached to a gold chain around her neck.

CHRISTINE
Think of it! (Spoken) **A secret engagement! Look – your future bride! Just think of it!**

RAOUL
But why is it secret? What have we to hide? You promised me.

CHRISTINE (nervously)
No, Raoul. Please don't. They'll see …

RAOUL

Well, then let them see. It's an engagement, not a crime!
Christine what are you afraid of?

CHRISTINE/RAOUL
Let's not argue …

CHRISTINE takes him by the arm.

CHRISTINE/RAOUL
Please pretend …

RAOUL
I can only hope I'll …

CHRISTINE
You will …

BOTH
… understand in time …

148. INT. FOYER – NIGHT

She pulls him into the dance to find the GUESTS in the midst of a frenzied waltz. CHRISTINE and RAOUL join the dance which becomes increasingly intense. As she spins, we see her POV, flashes of skull-like faces. The camera swoops down and over the GUESTS, spins within them and around them. The GUESTS are dancing up the horseshoe staircase into the upper foyers. CHRISTINE is dancing excitedly, but she keeps on glimpsing the vision of the fearful masks. She stops and leans on RAOUL's arm as the GUESTS march majestically back down either side of the staircase, converging in the centre, and down into the main foyer. RAOUL and CHRISTINE remain upstairs. The movement of the GUESTS is magnificent and a little eerie.

ALL
Masquerade! Paper faces on parade! Masquerade! Hide your face, so the world will never find you! Masquerade! Every face a different shade … Masquerade! Look around – there's another mask behind you! Masquerade! Burning glances, turning heads … Masquerade! Stop and stare at the sea of smiles around you! Masquerade! Grinning yellows, spinning reds … Masquerade! Take your fill – let the spectacle astound you!

But, at the height of the activity, MEG looks up and suddenly sees the terrifying reflection of the HUGE RED PHANTOM in the mirrored doors of the loge. She SCREAMS. A GROTESQUE FIGURE suddenly appears on the upper balcony, seven feet tall, dressed all in crimson, with a death's head. The PHANTOM has

come to the party. CHRISTINE and RAOUL, standing the other end of the balcony, are mesmerized. All are stunned and silent.

PHANTOM
Why so silent, good messieurs? Did you think that I had left you for good? Have you missed me, good messieurs? I have written you an opera!

He brandishes an enormous bound manuscript.

PHANTOM (CONT'D)
Here I bring the finished score – "Don Juan triumphant"!

And he throws it to ANDRE down below. Some pages fly. Besides MUSIC there are COSTUME and SET SKETCHES and PAINTINGS.

PHANTOM (CONT'D) (moving along the loge balcony)
Fondest greetings to you all, a few instructions just before the rehearsal starts: Carlotta must be taught to act …

CARLOTTA fumes.

PHANTOM (CONT'D)
… Not her normal trick of strutting round the stage. (looking down at Piangi) *Our Don Juan must lose some weight – it's not healthy in a man of Piangi's age!*

PIANGI fumes.

PHANTOM (CONT'D) (to the managers)
And my managers must learn that their place is in an office – not the arts!

ANDRE and FIRMIN fume.

He has reached the top of the grand staircase. On the same level, but far on the other side, stand RAOUL and CHRISTINE.

PHANTOM (CONT'D)
As for our star, Miss Christine Daae … (slow and sinister) *No doubt she'll do her best – it's true her voice is good. She knows, though, should she wish to excel, she has much still to learn, if pride will let her return to me, her teacher, her teacher …*

Magically, the lights dim, isolating the PHANTOM and CHRISTINE. Spellbound, the guests below watch as CHRISTINE and the PHANTOM descend their respective staircases, united by their music, moving ever closer towards each other until they arrive face to face on the mezzanine. She is mesmerized by him. The PHANTOM reaches out, grasps the chain that holds the secret engagement ring, and rips it from CHRISTINE's throat. RAOUL jumps between them. The PHANTOM turns on him furiously.

PHANTOM (CONT'D) (to CHRISTINE)
Your chains are still mine – you belong to me!

There is a FLASH AND A CLOUD OF SMOKE. The PHANTOM has disappeared down a trap door in the centre of the mezzanine. But RAOUL has seen the door in the smoke. In an instant, he leaps in after the PHANTOM as FIRMIN quips to ANDRE …

149. INT. PHANTOM'S WORLD/TRAP – NIGHT

The trap door snaps shut above him. RAOUL has landed in a box, a painted magic box and the walls are closing in on him. Just when it seems they may crush him, they fall away. RAOUL is in almost total darkness in a BRILLIANT and FIENDISHLY DESIGNED MAZE.

150. INT. PHANTOM'S WORLD/MAZE – NIGHT

We can make out a DEMONIC LABYRINTH. RAOUL catches a glimpse of a red cloak. He races after it, only to face A MIRROR. Shafts of light seep through cracks in the brickwork of the corridor. In each of these, RAOUL sees the red cloak whip through.
    RAOUL is catching up. ANOTHER MIRROR. He turns a corner, the PHANTOM is standing in front of him. RAOUL reaches him and touches the PHANTOM's shoulder. The

PHANTOM swivels. RAOUL is staring at the MANNEQUIN OF THE RED DEATH PHANTOM. He is unaware, however, that the noose of the Punjab Lasso is now hovering behind him. A hand reaches out and pulls RAOUL violently out of the way. The lasso whips harmlessly through the empty air. RAOUL turns to see who has saved him. MME. GIRY.

151. INT. PHANTOM'S WORLD/NARROW CORRIDOR – NIGHT

MME. GIRY is hurrying RAOUL through a more illuminated part of the corridor. Small gas lamps flicker in the gloom.

RAOUL
Madame Giry … Wait … !

MME. GIRY
Please, Monsieur, I know no more than anyone else.

RAOUL
That's not true!

MME. GIRY (uneasily)
Monsieur, don't ask … There have been too many accidents.

RAOUL
Accidents? Please Madame Giry, for all our sakes …

They have reached a door. MME. GIRY stops and looks at RAOUL. She looks back down the corridor. She is very frightened. But she decides to tell him.

MME. GIRY
Very well.

She quickly opens the door.

152. INT. MME. GIRY'S ROOM – NIGHT

This is MME. GIRY's little flat within the opera house. The furniture is tatty but there are posters of performances, ballet and opera memorabilia all around, the memories of her years at the Opera Populaire. She double-locks the door. RAOUL listens as MME. GIRY nervously begins telling her story.

MME. GIRY
It was years ago. There was a travelling fair in the city. Gypsies. I was very young.

RAOUL
Go on …

We are closing in on an old SEPIA PHOTOGRAPH of MME. GIRY as a twelve year old girl …

153. EXT./INT. FAIR – NIGHT (SEPIA) – FLASHBACK

…and see YOUNG GIRY accompanied by a dozen giggling BALLET GIRLS and escorted by a BALLET MISTRESS moving through a fair in a park under the shadow (MATTE) of the old opera house. (It is currently being renovated and is covered in scaffolding.)

The FAIR is a shabby, grimy affair, teeming with loutish, leering MEN, WHORES, GYPSIES, and DRUNKS who pester the BALLET GIRLS as they walk past. The tents and the banners proclaiming the various attractions flap in an eerie wind.

The general impression is one of innocence walking through a grotesque kind of hell. A LIVE MONKEY in Persian dress plays the tin cymbals as he scampers through the carnival delighting the young girls.

In one tent, they see a FORTUNE TELLER, a horrid TOOTHLESS WOMAN beckoning CLIENTS. A banner announces the "INCREDIBLE MAN-WOMAN".

In another tent, a flap is raised to reveal SIAMESE TWINS. YOUNG GIRY turns and sees a CONTORTIONIST, his back arched right back and his face, upside down, between his legs. He is laughing. They pass some horrible FREAKS abused by a huge, bearded OWNER with a bull-whip. Outside, FIRE EATERS, spit fire into the air. Some of the BALLET GIRLS are enjoying themselves. Not YOUNG GIRY; the place is grotesque, a nightmare. They approach one particular banner; "THE DEVIL'S CHILD" it announces. The MONKEY disappears under this banner as the vicious OWNER waves them to come in. His smile is disgusting. The BALLET GIRLS drag in YOUNG GIRY.

Inside, other CLIENTS are waiting. The BALLET GIRLS push to the front. YOUNG GIRY sees a cage. Inside, his head covered in a sack, a nine-year-old BOY is completing a beautifully delicate housing for a model monkey (a cruder version of the monkey we have already seen on the music box and who dances LIVE around him). The OWNER cracks his whip and is shouting at the BOY through the cage. The BOY is tied by ropes like a dog. He is obviously terrified, scrambling into the corner of his cage. The OWNER, letting fly with the whip, has entered the cage. He kicks the BOY's model and rips the sack off his head. We see the BOY's hand rise to his face, but the OWNER is still whipping him. Pathetically, the BOY's hands descend from his face. We do not see it. Instead, we see a look of shock and immense pity on YOUNG GIRY's face. Some of the other BALLET GIRLS are giggling insensitively.

The CLIENTS throw coins which land on the straw floor of the cage. We see the BOY crawl through the straw to retrieve the sack which he pulls back over his head.

YOUNG GIRY emerges from the tent and is hurried on by the other BALLET GIRLS and their MISTRESS. But YOUNG GIRY lingers. She looks back at the tent. Something draws her to it. She peers in, past the flapping canvas, and sees, inside the tent, the OWNER kicks the BOY out of the way and picks the money off the floor of the cage. The LIVE MONKEY shrieks. Suddenly, the BOY, with a Punjab Lasso fashioned with the ropes that bound him, strangles the OWNER. YOUNG GIRY watches the BOY garrotte his torturer. The evil man falls dead. The BOY looks up and sees YOUNG GIRY, just as a client coming into the tent screams. He frees himself and runs out of the tent. The two young people look at each other. Behind them, DOZENS OF PEOPLE arrive in the tent. YOUNG GIRY and the BOY hide in the shadows, breathless and terrified. He is clutching the CRUDE TOY MONKEY.

POLICEMEN with lanterns and GYPSIES with torches are closing in through the fair. She could turn him in but quickly, YOUNG GIRY tugs open a trap door at the foot of the opera house wall. She jumps in and the BOY leaps in after her, carrying his MONKEY AUTOMAT. The trap slams shut as POLICEMEN and GYPSIES run past above them.

154. INT. CHAPEL – NIGHT

YOUNG GIRY and the BOY jump into the tiny chapel. There is a second of gratitude in the YOUNG BOY's eyes but the aggressive shouting and running above forces YOUNG GIRY to push him into the safety of the bowels of the theatre. As he disappears into his new subterranean home, YOUNG GIRY kneels to pray.

END OF FLASHBACK (SEPIA SEQUENCE ENDS – BACK TO COLOUR)

155. INT. MME. GIRY's ROOM – NIGHT

And we are back with MME GIRY in her room with RAOUL.

MME. GIRY
He has known nothing else of life since then, except this Opera House. It was his playground and now his artistic domain … He is a genius! He's an architect and designer, he's a composer and a magician … A genius, Monsieur.

RAOUL
But, clearly, Madame Giry … genius has turned to madness.

166. INT./EXT. RAOUL/CAR – 1919 – BLACK AND WHITE – DUSK

RAOUL still in his car, breaks from his reverie to see his destination. His POV in the distance, A LEGENDARY OLD CEMETERY, in the fading light. HAUNTING MUSIC begins as we dissolve to:

167. INT. BALLET DORMITORY – 1870 – DAWN

AS THE FIRST RAY OF DAWN comes through CHRISTINE's transom window. CHRISTINE, in a robe, having not slept all night, makes a decision. She slowly opens the dressing room door.

168. INT. DORMITORY CORRIDOR – DAWN

RAOUL sleeps in a chair outside her door, his sword across his lap. CHRISTINE quietly tip-toes past him: careful not to wake him.

169. INT. STABLES – MOMENTS LATER – DAY

As the HAUNTING music builds, she quickly wakes one of the SLEEPING, DRUNKEN STABLE HANDS. But SOMEONE watches from the shadows, as CHRISTINE gives the STABLEMAN some money and leaves quickly.

STABLEMAN
Where to, mademoiselle?

CHRISTINE
The cemetery

170. INT. VAST COSTUME DEPARTMENT – DAY

Empty at dawn. CHRISTINE finds a black velvet dress and throws off her robe as her eyes focus on a vase of DARK RED ROSES.

171. INT. STABLES – DAY

The weary, bleary eyed, hungover STABLEMAN hitches horses to a carriage. As he finishes … THE DARK SHADOW moves swiftly and with one blow knocks him unconscious. As the STABLEMAN falls to the stable floor …

172. INT. DORMITORY CORRIDOR – DAY

RAOUL, outside CHRISTINE's door. Almost like a premonition, wakes.

173. INT. STABLES – SAME

CHRISTINE, dressed in a black velvet dress and cape, carrying the RED ROSES, gets in the OPEN CARRIAGE. She is unaware that the DRIVER, swathed in his black cloak, is not the STABLEMAN.

174. INT. DORMITORY (OR EXT. ROOFTOP) – DAY

RAOUL, holding his sword, hears the sound of horses' hooves on the cobbled streets and rushes to the window. He sees CHRISTINE's carriage disappearing into the grey dawn as snowflakes begin to fall.

175. INT. STABLES – DAY

RAOUL dashes into the stables to find the STABLEMAN starting to come to. He leaps bareback onto a WHITE STALLION.

176. EXT. PARIS STREETS – DAY

The OPEN CARRIAGE races down the snow-covered streets. It is cold and foggy. The horses hooves beat on the cobblestones, their nostrils smoke. The DRIVER swathed in black drives them on. CHRISTINE sits in the back, the wind presses her veil to her face like a mask.

CHRISTINE (V.O.)
In sleep he sang to me, in dreams he came …
That voice which calls to me and speaks my name …

176A. EXT. PARIS STREETS – DAY

Raoul with sword riding white charger.

177. EXT. CEMETERY – DAY

A sweeping shot of the huge LEGENDARY CEMETERY shrouded in mist. CLOSE on a bell tolling. We WIDEN to find CHRISTINE, bearing the bouquet of red roses, gliding past towering MAUSOLEUMS and CROSSES. Great GARGOYLES and ANGELS stare down at her. In the distance, the carriage and horses disappear into the fog.

CHRISTINE
Little Lotte thought of everything and nothing … Her father promised her that he would send her the Angel of Music … Her father promised her … Her father promised her …
In the distance, we see a large mausoleum on a ridge. CHRISTINE is clearly moving toward it. We see her through the passing statues and crosses. She lowers her hood and veil.

CHRISTINE (CONT'D)
You were once my one companion … You were all that mattered … You were once a friend and father – then my world was shattered … Wishing you were somehow here again … Wishing you were somehow near … Sometimes it seemed, if I just dreamed, somehow you would be here …

CHRISTINE is unaware of the LONG DARK SHADOWS sweeping across the snow towards her.

CHRISTINE (CONT'D)
Wishing I could hear your voice again … Knowing that I never would … Dreaming of you won't help me to do all that I dreamed I could … Passing bells and sculpted angels cold and monumental seem, for you, the wrong companions – you were warm and gentle.

CHRISTINE is arriving at the foot of the mausoleum steps.

CHRISTINE (CONT'D)
Too many years fighting back tears … Why can't the past just die … ? Wishing you were somehow here again … Knowing we must say goodbye … Try to forgive … Teach me to live … Give me the strength to try …

The camera swoops down and up over CHRISTINE.

CHRISTINE (CONT'D)
No more memories, no more silent tears … no more gazing across the wasted years … Help me say goodbye. Help me say goodbye.

She kneels down and lays the red roses on the snow-covered steps. High above her, the gates at the top of the steps begin to open. We HEAR the PHANTOM'S VOICE from deep within the golden candlelit crypt.

PHANTOM (O.S) (very soft and enticing)
Wandering child … so lost … so helpless … yearning for my guidance …

Bewildered, CHRISTINE looks up. She sees that the mausoleum's inner gates are open; a strange glow emanates from the interior. Lights spills down the steps. She murmurs breathlessly:

CHRISTINE
Angel … or father … friend … or Phantom …? Who is it there staring … ?

PHANTOM (O.S.) (more and more hypnotic)
Have you forgotten your angel … ?

CHRISTINE
Angel … oh, speak … what endless longings echo in this whisper!

She rises slowly, drawn to the light above her.

PHANTOM (O.S.)
Too long you've wandered in winter … far from my fathering gaze …

CHRISTINE is slowly ascending the steps towards the inner doors and light.

CHRISTINE (increasingly mesmerized)
Wildly my mind beats against you …

PHANTOM (O.S.)
You resist …

CHRISTINE	PHANTOM
… yet the soul obeys	*yet the soul obeys …*
Angel of Music I	*Angel of Music! You*
denied you …	*denied me …*
turning from	*turning from*
true beauty …	*true beauty …*
Angel of Music!	*Angel of Music!*
My protector	*Do not shun me …*
Come to me,	*Come to your*
strange angel …	*strange angel …*

We have begun to discern a dark form within the light of the mausoleum.

PHANTOM (O.S.) (beckoning her)
I am your Angel of Music … Come to me: Angel of Music …

178. EXT. CEMETERY – DAY

But, just as CHRISTINE reaches the last few steps, RAOUL, on the magnificent white charger, leaps over the wall of the cemetery with a great cry.

Inexorably, the PHANTOM continues to beckon CHRISTINE.

CHRISTINE is now at the entrance to the mausoleum. RAOUL meanwhile is galloping and jumping through the crosses and over the monuments. Snow and dirt fly.

RAOUL (shouting)
Whatever you may believe, this man ... this thing ... is not your father!

Coming out of her trance, CHRISTINE turns:

CHRISTINE
Raoul ...

And sees RAOUL arriving on the white charger. At last, the PHANTOM appears up on the top of the mausoleum behind the huge stone cross.

The PHANTOM flies at RAOUL, his sword drawn. What ensues is a spectacular fight through the cemetery. RAOUL fights desperately, managing to match the PHANTOM in swordplay, displaying bravery, skill and courage ... CHRISTINE screams as the PHANTOM forces RAOUL back. The PHANTOM laughs as he slashes at RAOUL, cutting him on the shoulder. But RAOUL is a fine swordsman and fights on, parrying the PHANTOM's blows and gradually forcing the PHANTOM himself back. As he pushes the PHANTOM back, the PHANTOM falls against the stone side of the mausoleum. RAOUL is close to having the opportunity to run the PHANTOM through with his sword. He looks into the PHANTOM's eyes – they burn with hatred.

CHRISTINE
No!! Raoul .... no .... Not like this.

RAOUL looks to CHRISTINE for a split second. RAOUL remounts his horse and sweeps CHRISTINE up onto the saddle beside him.

PHANTOM
Now let it be war upon you both!

As they ride off, we notice a trail of blood red rose petals scattered in the snow. WE DISSOLVE TO:

179. EXT. SAME CEMETERY – 1919 – DUSK (BLACK AND WHITE)

RAOUL reaches for the spot on his arm where the memory of the <u>OLD WOUND</u> still exists. He looks up to see a <u>LEGION OF GENDARME</u> MARCHING PAST. As he watches them march away, we stay with their BACKS as they MORPH INTO.

180. EXT. OPERA POPULAIRE – NIGHT

GENDARMES from 1870 (BACK TO COLOUR) They hurry up the OPEN STEPS, past large posters announcing "GRAND PREMIERE – DON JUAN TRIUMPHANT!"

181. INT. STABLES/BACKSTAGE – SAME

More GENDARMES enter the backstage area via the stables, shouldering weapons. They march through the chaotic preparations for the show as REYER rehearses PIANGI and CARLOTTA.

RAOUL
We have all been blind. And yet the answer is staring us in the face. This could be the chance to ensnare our clever friend.

ANDRE
We're listening …

FIRMIN
go on …

RAOUL
We shall play his game – perform his work – but remember we hold the ace … For, if Miss Daae sings, he is certain to attend …

ANDRE (carried along by the idea)
We are certain the doors are barred …

FIRMIN (likewise)
We are certain the police are there … we are certain they're armed …

RAOUL/ANDRE/FIRMIN (savouring their victory)
The curtain falls, his reign will end!

RAOUL notices CHRISTINE watching from the wings. Her look; accusation and fear. She turns and runs from him.

RAOUL follows to …

181A. THE CHAPEL
(OR THE WINGS—NEED TO REHEARSE) – CONTINUOUS

Where he finds her kneeling near her father's memorial. Candles burn on the altar, bathing her in a soft light.

CHRISTINE (spoken)
Raoul, I'm frightened – don't make me do this … Raoul, it scares me – don't put me through this ordeal by fire … He'll take me, I know … We'll be parted forever … He won't let me go … What I once used to dream I now dread… If he finds me, it won't ever end … (sung) *And he'll always be there,*

singing songs in my head … He'll always be there, singing songs in my head …

RAOUL (to CHRISTINE)
You said yourself he was nothing but a man … Yet while he lives, he will haunt us till we're dead …

CHRISTINE turns away, unhappily.

CHRISTINE
Twisted every way, what answer can I give? Am I to risk my life, to win the chance to live? Can I betray the man who once inspired my voice? Do I become his prey? Do I have any choice? He kills without a thought, he murders all that's good … I know I can't refuse, and yet, I wish I could. Oh God – if I agree, what horrors wait for me in this – the Phantom's Opera … ?

RAOUL (very tenderly)
Christine, Christine, don't think that I don't care – but every hope and every prayer rests on <u>you</u> now …

CHRISTINE, overcome by her conflicting emotions, buries her head in her hands. We see the picture of CHRISTINE's FATHER on his memorial. RAOUL takes her head in his hand and kisses her as we dissolve through CANDLE FLAME TO …

155A. INT. PHANTOM's LAIR – NIGHT

Surrounded by drawings and paintings of CHRISTINE, the PHANTOM sings of loneliness and unrequited love.

155B. INT. PHANTOM'S LAIR – CONTINUOUS

By candlelight, the PHANTOM prepares for his finale: we see INTIMATE extreme CLOSE-UPS of his elaborate MAQUILLAGE. Without revealing what he looks like underneath, WE SEE THE BLACK WIG secured from the back. THE MASK in place. STILL FROM THE BACK … Elaborate stage makeup covers what the mask doesn't.

PHANTOM (V.O.)
Seal my fate tonight – I hate to have to cut the fun short, but the joke's wearing thin … Let the audience in … Let my opera begin!

He rises now. Ready for his "PREMIERE"…As he passes his MINIATURE THEATRE with the MINIATURE SET he has designed for "Don Juan"… He snatches CHRISTINE's figure into his grasp.

PHANTOM
Let the audience in … !

He throws one of his many CANDLES into the SMALL STAGE and it bursts into FLAME. The other WAX FIGURES MELT.

PHANTOM (CONT'D)
Let my opera begin!!!

CAMERA moves into THE MOLTEN FIGURES … as we DISSOLVE TO:

183. INT. AUDITORIUM – NIGHT

Painted FLAMES on red velvet curtains of the real theatre. CAMERA WIDENS to reveal … The AUDIENCE are taking their seats for the premiere of "Don Juan Triumphant".

184. INT. FOYER – NIGHT

MONTAGE to show that the armed SOLDIERS and GENDARMES have taken over the building. Supervised by RAOUL, ANDRE and FIRMIN, all exits from the opera house are barred and sealed as the last of the audience filters into the auditorium.

185. INT. BACKSTAGE – NIGHT

The AUDIENCE is locked in. SOLDIERS guard all exits. Backstage, STAGEHANDS, SINGERS and DANCERS are preparing for the impending performance, watched by the SOLDIERS.

(Just another chance for young people to flirt – especially TOOTHY TART and SEXY CHORUS GIRL.)

186. INT. AUDITORIUM – NIGHT

Meanwhile, the ORCHESTRA has been tuning up. REYER takes his bow on his podium to polite applause. He raises his baton. The overture begins.

It is incredibly dissonant, a cacophony of sound; the AUDIENCE has never heard anything like it before. People are horrified, consult their programmes, cough and whisper, fidget uncomfortably. SOMEONE tries to leave but the doors are locked. REYER, pained by the music he is forced to conduct, stuffs cotton plugs into his ears. The RED CURTAIN rises.

187. INT. STAGE – NIGHT

The awesome set, modern and severe, is dominated by two Moorish pillars with stairs supporting a high balcony. Below, a pit of silk flames. Scrims hang from the flies. CHORUS, including MEG as a gypsy whore and CARLOTTA as a hag, and DANCERS (EIGHT MEN/EIGHT WOMEN), dressed in gypsy peasant, lusty style. The atmosphere is dark and erotic. MEG disappears into DON JUAN's bedroom (part of the inn on stage).

CHORUS
Here the sire may serve the dam, here the master takes his meat! Here the sacrificial lamb utters one despairing bleat!

CARLOTTA moves centre stage dressed and made-up like a whorish hag; tatty clothes, bad wig, a wart with hair growing from it. However, she is still the reigning diva of the Opera Populaire and makes the most of her bit part.

CARLOTTA and CHORUS
Poor young maiden! For the thrill on your tongue of stolen sweets, you will have to pay the bill – tangled in the winding sheets! Serve the meal and serve the maid! Serve the master so that, when tables, plans and maids are laid Don Juan triumphs once again!

MEG is supposed to enter from the inn with a purse of money earned from DON JUAN. But, CARLOTTA milks her only moment ("AGAIN!") for as long as possible, keeping MEG half-coming and half-going. Finally, CARLOTTA finishes and MEG skips across the stage as SIGNOR PIANGI as DON JUAN appears from the inn and grabs his servant.

DON JUAN (PIANGI)
Passarino, faithful friend, once again recite the plan.

PASSARINO
Your young guest believes I'm you – I, the master, you, the man.

DON JUAN (PIANGI)
When you met, you wore my cloak, she could not have seen your face. She believes she dines with me in her master's borrowed place! Furtively, we'll scoff and quaff, stealing what, in truth, is mine. When it's late and modesty starts to mellow, with the wine …

PASSARINO
You come home! I use your voice – slam the door like crack of doom!

DON JUAN (PIANGI)
I shall cry, "Come, hide with me! Where, oh, where? Of course – my room!"

PASSARINO
Poor thing hasn't got a chance!

DON JUAN (PIANGI)
Here's my hat, my cloak and sword. Conquest is assured, if I do not forget myself and laugh …

Laughing, DON JUAN puts on PASSARINO's clothes, wrapping the cloak around him and covering his head with the hood. (NOTE: more Goya than Grim Reaper). He strides upstage and disappears behind the scrims. BUT HE IS NOT ALONE. When we next see DON JUAN, it will be the PHANTOM. Meanwhile, a sensual gypsy-girl, AMINTA (CHRISTINE), enters.

AMINTA (CHRISTINE)
"… no thoughts within her head, but thoughts of joy! no dreams within her heart, but dreams of love!"

PASSARINO
Master?

DON JUAN replies upstage:

DON JUAN (PHANTOM)
Passarino – go away! For the trap is set and waits for its prey …

PASSARINO exits.

The PHANTOM, disguised as DON JUAN pretending to be PASSARINO, is standing downstage. He now wears PIANGI's robe, his face hidden by the cowl. The scrims lift as he moves downstage toward CHRISTINE. CHORUS and DANCERS leave the stage.
PHANTOM

You have come here in pursuit of your deepest urge, in pursuit of that wish, which till now has been silent, silent … I have brought you, that our passions may fuse and merge – in your mind you've already succumbed to me, dropped all defences, completely succumbed to me – now you are here with me: no second thoughts, you've decided, decided …

The PHANTOM is now half-way towards CHRISTINE. The SILHOUETTES of MALE DANCERS appear behind him. Moving erotically in shadow and silhouette.

PHANTOM
Past the point of no return – no backward glances: our games of make-believe are at an end … Past all thought of "if" or "when" – no use resisting: abandon thought and let the dream descend … What raging fire shall flood the soul? What rich desire unlocks its door? What sweet seduction lies before us? Past the point of no return, the final threshold – what warm, unspoken secrets will we learn beyond the point of no return …

The PHANTOM has arrived downstage right. The MALE DANCERS disappear. He slowly begins to ascend the stairs leading up to the balcony. CHRISTINE, downstage left, now sings alone.

CHRISTINE
You have brought me to that moment where words run dry, to that moment where speech disappears into silence, silence … I have come here, hardly knowing the reason why … In my mind I've already imagined our bodies entwining, defenceless and silent – Now I am here with you: no second thoughts, I've decided, decided …

The SILHOUETTES of VOLUPTUOUS FEMALE DANCERS appear behind her, moving erotically in shadow.

CHRISTINE
Past the point of no return – no going back now: our passion-play has now, at last, begun …

She starts up the stairs on her side.

CHRISTINE (CONT'D)
Past all thought of right or wrong – one final question: how long should we two wait, before we're one … ?

Both CHRISTINE and the PHANTOM are on the balcony. Slowly they walk toward each other.

CHRISTINE (CONT'D)
When will the blood begin to race, the sleeping bud burst into bloom? When will the flames at last consume us … ?

188. INT. WINGS/STAGE – NIGHT

The pillars of the set swivel isolating CHRISTINE and the PHANTOM from the ground. The PHANTOM's trap is sprung. RAOUL and soldiers appear in the <u>WINGS</u>. There is no way of reaching the balcony. The PHANTOM and CHRISTINE are face to face.

BOTH
Past the point of no return, the final threshold – the bridge is crossed, so stand and watch it burn ... We've passed the point of no return ...

Very slowly, the entire set starts to REVOLVE. Up on the set balcony, the PHANTOM is holding and caressing CHRISTINE.

PHANTOM
Say you'll share with me one love, one lifetime ... Lead me, save me from my solitude ... Say you want me with you here beside you ... Anywhere you go, let me go too – Christine, that's all I ask of ...

We never reach the word "you", for CHRISTINE quite calmly removes the PHANTOM's cowl, mask and wig. For the first time, everyone sees the whole of the PHANTOM's horrifying skull. At the same time, the REVOLVE has revealed PIANGI hanging by the neck from the set. Screams.

POLICEMEN, STAGEHANDS, rush onto the stage in confusion. Also: ANDRE, FIRMIN, RAOUL, MME. GIRY, CARLOTTA and MEG. Screams and gunshots. The PHANTOM <u>CUTS</u> one of the many massive <u>TASSELLED ROPES</u> that are part of the set design.

189. INT. STAGE – AUDITORIUM – NIGHT

<u>THE HUGE CHANDELIER CRASHES TO THE STALLS BELOW.</u> Mass DEVASTATION and PANDEMONIUM ... the theatre bursts into flame. The AUDIENCE stampedes for the doors.

190. INT.WINGS/STAGE – NIGHT

Very fast: the PHANTOM grabs CHRISTINE and jumps from the balcony into the fire below. In the confusion, a scrim catches

fire. PIANGI is cut down from his gibbet.

ANDRE
Oh my God!

FIRMIN
We're ruined, Andre – ruined!

191. INT. PHANTOM'S WORLD/UNDERGROUND LOCK – NIGHT

The PHANTOM has CHRISTINE in the boat. The lock which leads down to the PHANTOM's lair descends, revealing the portcullis and the lagoon.

PHANTOM
Down once more to the dungeons of my black despair! Down we plunge to the prison of my mind! Down that path into darkness deep as hell! (He pauses for a moment, rounding on her bitterly) *Why, you ask, was I bound and chained in this cold and dismal place? Not for any mortal sin, but the wickedness of my abhorrent face!*

192. INT. STAGE/AUDITORIUM – NIGHT

MONTAGE of shots showing the chaos in the opera house. GENDARMES and BACKSTAGE CREW trying to put out the fire.

193. INT. BACKSTAGE – NIGHT

Through the smoke, SOLDIERS and STAGEHANDS are rushing down corridors, up and down staircases.

CHORUS
Track down this murderer! He must be found! Track down this murderer! He must be found!

194. INT. PHANTOM'S LAIR – NIGHT

The portcullis comes down behind the boat. The curtain closes. The PHANTOM guides the boat to the shore.

PHANTOM
Hounded out by everyone! Met with hatred everywhere! No kind words from anyone! No compassion anywhere!

He drags CHRISTINE out of the boat and throws her to the ground.

PHANTOM (CONT'D)
Christine, Christine, why, why … ?

195. INT. PHANTOM'S WORLD – CORRIDOR – NIGHT

RAOUL and MME. GIRY are making their way down the corridor.

195A. INT. PHANTOM'S WORLD – NIGHT

RAOUL and MME. GIRY follow the staircase down past the stables.

195B. INT. PHANTOM'S WORLD – CORRIDOR/BRIDGE – NIGHT

A pack of rats slithers over RAOUL and MME. GIRY's feet. She raises her hands again.

MME. GIRY
Your hand at the level of your eyes!

RAOUL
… at the level of your eyes …

The gargoyles seem to sing mockingly:

VOICE (O.S.)
Your hand at the level of your eyes …

MME. GIRY
This is as far as I dare go.
They have reached a bridge which stretches out into the gloom. It has no sides. RAOUL rips off his tailcoat and neckwear. The shoulder wound begins to bleed through his white shirt.

RAOUL
Thank you.

She makes the sign of a cross and goes. RAOUL gingerly steps onto the bridge. Half-way across, the stones under his feet suddenly give way. RAOUL plummets downward. He falls and falls through the darkness …

196. INT. PHANTOM'S WORLD/UNDERGROUND CANAL – NIGHT

RAOUL lands in the water of the canal. (Poss. POV INTO WATER?) Twisting and turning, he drops down into the murky depths. He re-surfaces gasping for air. He looks up and, to his horror, a grill is descending towards him.

197. INT. BACKSTAGE/FLIES/CORRIDORS – NIGHT

MONTAGE of shots showing the chaos still reigning in the opera house. Smoke and flames everywhere. SOLDIERS rush through the backstage areas past panicking DANCERS and SINGERS.

198. INT. PHANTOM'S WORLD/UNDERGROUND CANAL – NIGHT

RAOUL cannot find any escape from the grill which is now pushing his head down into the water. His fingers clutch the ironwork and disappear into the depths. He is going to die. We see him struggling underwater with the grill above. He swims desperately to find a way out.

Suddenly, an iron wall appears in the gloom. Next to it, fixed to the brick wall of the canal, RAOUL find a gear. He wrenches it down. Above, we see the water level subside. RAOUL has found the gear of the PHANTOM's lock. His head re-appears above the water.

199. INT. PHANTOM's LAIR – NIGHT

CHRISTINE rounds fiercely on the PHANTOM. The PHANTOM tears her dress off, the costume from "Don Juan".

CHRISTINE
Have you gorged yourself at last, in your lust for blood?
(No reply) *Am I now to be prey to your lust for flesh?*

PHANTOM (coldly)
That fate which condemns me to wallow in blood, has also denied me the joys of the flesh ... This face – the infection which poisons our love ...

He takes the bridal veil from her MANNEQUIN and moves slowly toward her. She turns away.

PHANTOM (CONT'D) (very quietly and darkly)
This face which earned a mother's fear and loathing ... A mask, my first unfeeling scrap of clothing ...

And places the veil on her head.

PHANTOM (CONT'D)
Pity comes too late – turn around and face your fate:

He turns her round.

PHANTOM (CONT'D)
An eternity of <u>this</u> before your eyes!

CHRISTINE rips the veil from her head and throws it to the ground. She then proceeds to tear the canvas covers off the mirrors surrounding them, revealing hundreds of reflections of her and PHANTOM.

CHRISTINE
This haunted face holds no horror for me now ... It's in your soul that the true distortion lies.

200. INT. PHANTOM'S LAIR – NIGHT

A stunned silence. Meanwhile, the curtains which hide the portcullis have parted to reveal RAOUL behind, knee deep in water. The PHANTOM turns:

PHANTOM
Wait! I think, my dear, we have a guest! Sir ...

CHRISTINE (seeing Raoul, stunned)
Raoul ... !

PHANTOM (to RAOUL, with a mock-courteous bow)
... this is indeed an unparalleled delight! I had rather hoped that you would come. And now, my wish comes true – you have truly made my night!

CHRISTINE (to PHANTOM)
Let me go.

RAOUL (pleading, grasping the bars of the gate)
Free her! do what you like, only free her! have you no pity?

PHANTOM (to CHRISTINE dryly)
Your lover makes a passionate plea!

CHRISTINE
Please, Raoul, it's useless ...

RAOUL
I love her! Does that mean nothing? I love her! Show some compassion ...

PHANTOM (snarls furiously at RAOUL)
The world showed no compassion to me!

RAOUL (calming)
Christine ... Christine ... (to the Phantom) *Let me see her.*

PHANTOM (dry again)
Be my guest, sir ...

The Phantom pulls a lever and the portcullis rises enough to allow RAOUL to stagger in.

PHANTOM
Monsieur, I bid you welcome! Did you think that I would harm her? Why would I make her pay for the sins which are yours ... ?

Like lightening, the Punjab Lasso cracks through the air and, before RAOUL has a chance to move, catches him by the neck. He is jerked high into the air and down onto a stool. All the PHANTOM has to do is kick the stool away.

PHANTOM (CONT'D) (taunting)
Order your fine horses now! Raise up your hand to the level of your eyes! Nothing can save you now – except perhaps Christine –

He turns to her and thrusts the veil and wedding gown into her hands.

PHANTOM (CONT'D)
Start a new life with me – buy his freedom with your love! Refuse me, and you send your lover to his death! This is the choice – this is the point of no return!

CHRISTINE (to the PHANTOM)
The tears I might have shed for your dark fate grow cold and turns to tears of hate …

Looking at RAOUL, she places the veil on her head and begins putting on the wedding gown. ALL THREE pause for a moment. RAOUL breaks the moment with:

RAOUL
Christine, forgive me, please forgive me … I did it all for you … and all for nothing …

CHRISTINE (looking at the PHANTOM but to herself)
Farewell, my fallen idol and false friend … We had such hopes, and now those hopes are shattered …

PHANTOM (to CHRISTINE)
Too late for turning back, too late for prayers and useless pity …

RAOUL (to CHRISTINE)
Say you love him, and my life is over!

PHANTOM
All hope of cries of help: no point in fighting … For either way you choose, You cannot win!

RAOUL
Either way you choose, he has to win …

PHANTOM
So do you end your days with me, or do you send him to his grave?

RAOUL (to PHANTOM)
Why make her lie to you to save me?

PHANTOM
Past the point of no return –

CHRISTINE
Angel of Music …

RAOUL
For pity's sake, Christine, say no!

CHRISTINE
… Who deserved this?

PHANTOM
… the final threshold …

RAOUL
Don't throw your life away for my sake …

PHANTOM
His life is now the prize which you must earn!

CHRISTINE
Why do you curse mercy?

RAOUL
I fought so hard to free you …

CHRISTINE
Angel of Music …

PHANTOM
You've passed the point of no return …

CHRISTINE
… you deceived me – I gave you my mind blindly …

A pause. The PHANTOM looks coldly at CHRISTINE. She is now standing in her wedding gown.

PHANTOM
You try my patience – make your choice!
He holds up the ring he tore from her neck. It is on the stem of a RED ROSE with BLACK RIBBON.

CHRISTINE (quietly at first, then with growing emotion)
Pitiful creature of darkness … what kind of life have you known … ? God give me courage to show you you are not alone!

She calmly puts the ring on her finger and kisses him full on the lips. She pulls away, tears streaming down her cheeks. The PHANTOM is stunned. Then, she leans toward him and embraces him again. But this time the kiss is long and deep. A lover's kiss. As it ends, they look straight into each others' eyes. The PHANTOM is crying, devastated. He has never known human love. CHRISTINE's gesture – her sacrifice and at the

same time commitment – are too much for this tragic man to bear. Suddenly, he moves. The rope suspending RAOUL falls harmlessly to the ground. He addresses RAOUL as he jerks the lever which raises the portcullis.

CHORUS (out of shot)
Track down this murderer – he must be found! Hunt out this animal who runs to ground! Too long he's preyed on us – but now we know: the Phantom of the Opera is there, deep down below … Who is this monster, this murdering beast? Revenge for Piangi! Revenge for Buquet! This creature must never go free …

PHANTOM
Take her – forget me – forget all of this … Leave me alone – forget all you've seen … Go now – don't let them find you! Take the boat – swear to me never to tell the secret you know of the angel in hell – go … go now … go now and leave me!

And he runs up into the BLACK SWAN bedroom.

We INTERCUT with:

201. INT. PHANTOM'S WORLD – CORRIDOR – NIGHT

MEG is leading the torch-carrying MOB down into the PHANTOM's lair.

201B. INT. PHANTOM'S WORLD – CORRIDOR/ BRIDGE – NIGHT

Flaming timbers and hot coals fall from the opera house above into the underground canal. They are getting closer and closer.

202. INT. PHANTOM'S LAIR/BEDROOM – NIGHT

The PHANTOM looks at the monkey musical box and listens.

PHANTOM (to the musical box)
Masquerade … Paper faces on parade … Masquerade …Hide your face, so the world will never find you …

He turns and sees CHRISTINE standing at the bedroom door. His look is of immense longing and helplessness. She walks slowly toward him.

PHANTOM (whispered)
Christine, I love you …

She stands before him and we think she's going to stay but instead she takes off her ring and places it on his finger. She hurries off. The PHANTOM stares at the ring on his finger. We stay on him as he hears:

CHRISTINE (in the distance)
Say you'll share with me one love, one lifetime …

RAOUL
Say the word, and I will follow you …

203. INT. PHANTOM'S LAIR/CANAL – NIGHT

The PHANTOM comes out of the bedroom and sees, through the descending grill, the boat disappearing into the darkness of the underground canal. CHRISTINE is looking back at him. She seems to be singing for him.

CHRISTINE
Share each day with me … each night … each morning …
She disappears still looking at him.

PHANTOM (looking after her)
You alone can make my song take flight – it's over now, the music of the night …

He smashes all the mirrors around the lair and sets fire to his world. He turns and sees the MOB with their torches approaching along the CANAL. The PHANTOM walks slowly towards his throne and sits on it, gathering his cloak around him, surrounded by shattered images and the burning lair.

The MOB stops at the portcullis. MEG dives down into the water and comes up the other side. The PHANTOM has entirely covered himself with the cloak. MEG crosses to the throne and, tentatively but courageously, pulls the cloak away revealing empty air. The PHANTOM has vanished, leaving only his WHITE MASK. In wonder, she reaches out and picks up the mask in her small hand.

CAMERA moves into the BLACK EYE HOLE OF THE MASK as we DISSOLVE to RAOUL'S EYE … 1919 (BLACK AND WHITE)

204. EXT. CEMETERY 1919 – DUSK

CAMERA widens to see the NURSE and DRIVER wheeling RAOUL through. They stop. With great effort and the assistance of his companions RAOUL stands and slowly takes a few steps to a MAGNIFICENT MONUMENT. EMBEDDED in the MARBLE is an oval PORTRAIT OF CHRISTINE at her peak. The stone reads: CHRISTINE: THE COUNTESS OF CHAGNY. BELOVED WIFE AND MOTHER.

RAOUL shakes off his companions as he takes the MONKEY and slowly places it amid the beautiful flowers at her grave. He begins to turn away, when something catches his eye. although the film remains BLACK AND WHITE – IN VIVID COLOR A SINGLE RED ROSE lies at the foot of the monument, with a BLACK RIBBON. RAOUL's face pales as the mystery continues … for as the camera ZOOMS SLOWLY to the RED ROSE … we see THE RING that CHRISTINE gave the PHANTOM years ago. IT SPARKLES ON THE STEM.

THE END.

First published in Great Britain in 2004 by
PAVILION BOOKS
The Chrysalis Building, Bramley Road,
London W10 6SP

An imprint of **Chrysalis** Books Group plc

Designer: Nigel Soper
Associate Publisher: Kate Oldfield
Editor: Katherine Morton
Editorial Assistant: Kate Burkhalter

A CIP catalogue record for this book is available from the British
Library.

ISBN: 1 86205 691 9

Text set in Garamond
Colour origination by Anorax Imaging Ltd, Leeds
Printed and bound in France by Partenaires Fabrication

10 9 8 7 6 5 4 3 2 1

This book can be ordered direct from the publisher. Please contact
the marketing department, but try your bookshop first.

All photography by Alex Bailey

Additional photography by Stephen F. Morley and Stuart Hendry.

© Really Useful Films, 2004
© Scion Films Phantom Productions Partnership, 2004

with the exception of:

1T Roger-Viollet/Rex; **9** Designed by Dewynters/The Really Useful
Group; **10–11** Universal/The Kobal Collection; **13–15** Roger-
Viollet/Rex; **17–18** Universal/The Kobal Collection; **20** Universal/BFI;
21 Universal/The Kobal Collection; **22–24** Clive Barda/Arena Pal; **26**
Redcase Ltd./Maria Björnson; **27** Clive Barda/Arena Pal; **28** Redcase
Ltd./Maria Bjornson; **29** Clive Barda/Arena Pal; **30** Colin Willoughby;
31–42L Clive Barda/Arena Pal; **42R–43** Michael Le Poer Trench; **44–45**
Clive Barda/Arena Pal.